WALK
THE WALK
and
TALK
THE TALK

WALK
THE WALK
and
TALK
THE TALK

*An Ethnography of a
Drug Abuse Treatment Facility*

Geoffrey R. Skoll

TEMPLE UNIVERSITY PRESS
Philadelphia

Temple University Press, Philadelphia 19122
Copyright © 1992 by Temple University. All rights reserved
Published 1992
Printed in the United States of America

⊗ The paper used in this publication meets the minimum requirements of
American National Standard for Information Sciences—
Permanence of Paper for
Printed Library Materials, ANSI Z39.48-
1984

Library of Congress Cataloging-in-Publication Data
Skoll, Geoffrey R., 1948–
    Walk the walk and talk the talk : an ethnography of a drug abuse
treatment facility / Geoffrey R. Skoll.
        p.   cm.
    Includes bibliographical references.
    ISBN 0-87722-917-1
    1. Narcotic addicts—Rehabilitation—United States.   2. Drug abuse
counseling—Social aspects—United States.   3. Drug abuse
counselors—United States—Biography.   4. Skoll, Geoffrey R., 1948–.
I. Title.
HV5825.S54   1992
362.29'185'0973—dc20   91-34771

To Kathy

CONTENTS

ACKNOWLEDGMENTS

I AM DEEPLY indebted to Professor William Washabaugh (a.k.a. John Doe) and to Professors Edward Wellin and Eleanor Miller, upon whose support I relied throughout this project. I also wish to thank Professors Lynne Goldstein and Bernard Gendron. I am grateful to my analyst, Michael Tomaro, for helping me to keep sane during the fieldwork. Needless to say, the research could not have been conducted without the forebearance of the residents and staff of the drug treatment facility. Michael Ames, editor-in-chief of Temple University Press, has been of immeasurable assistance in helping to turn this manuscript into a book. Finally, I want to express my deepest, heartfelt gratitude to Kathy, without whose unswerving support I would not have attempted this work.

NOTE ON PUNCTUATION

Double quotation marks (" ") are used for terms and jargon peculiar to the drug treatment center. Single quotation marks (' ') signify emphasis or special usage.

WALK
THE WALK
and
TALK
THE TALK

CHAPTER 1

Introduction

I WAS INTRODUCED to the residential drug treatment facility that I shall call DTF when I applied for a job as a counselor. I was familiar with more or less equivalent establishments for people who have become mentally ill (a formal, administrative designation, not necessarily meant to be descriptive). In such places, typically called "group homes," there is a pervasive atmosphere of depression, in no small part aided by the administration of major tranquilizers. Here, at DTF, it seemed as if everyone were energized. People were talking and shouting as they swept floors and moved furniture. Everyone seemed to have something important to do and was intent on doing it. Later I learned that I had arrived during an event known as a "tighten-up," or general clean-up, that occurs three or four times a day. While I waited for the interview, several residents asked if I was there for the counselor job and wanted to know what I thought of the place. I remember thinking that the people were very much *alive*, in contrast to so many other people in residential treatment.

My first day on the job included participation in a group meeting that was a combination welcome to me and farewell to a departing counselor. During her farewell address to the assembled residents, the departing counselor tossed around a large ball of yarn to the circle of seated residents so that each resident held onto the string, and the counselor received the ball back from each resident. This yarn, she said, symbolized her ongoing ties with everyone there and the ties that each resident had to the others. I remember thinking, "No one really believes this."

When it came to the introduction part of the meeting, all the residents identified themselves by name and status in the program—that is, what level or stage they were at in the program of treatment. Each one also told me that the reason s/he was there was to get to be drug and crime free. I later learned this was a ritualistic phrase that the residents said to each other every morning.

I have always believed that initial encounters are important stage-setting devices and often are uniquely revealing about subsequent developments in human relationships. That belief, in conjunction with the highly emotive atmosphere created by the departing counselor's farewell performance, made me feel very much "on the spot"—that I had to say just the right thing and with the right tone of voice. And perhaps the most important thing to me at the moment was to try to get back down to earth and away from what seemed remarkably maudlin sentimentality. Therefore, after I told the residents my name and gave some of my professional background, I told them that the reason I was there was that I was getting paid. As it turned out, what I said at that moment of introduction had little consequence for my status with respect to the residents, principally because resident turnover was so high that within a few months hardly any member of that welcoming group remained in the facility.

I had already decided that I could not pass up my presence in DTF as a research opportunity, and discussed it with the staff, who encouraged me to analyze "the culture" (as the director put it) of DTF. So, after telling the residents that I was there because I was getting paid for it, I told them that I also intended to engage in social-scientific research and that I hoped that I could learn a lot from them.

I was concerned that my professional distancing, my research goals, and the concomitant denial of personal and emotional involvement would put the residents on the defensive and establish insurmountable barriers to the kind of rapport necessary for both therapy and participant-observation research. As I began to be socialized to the role of counselor, I realized that my worry about distancing myself was misplaced. Part of being a counselor at DTF seemed to imply the adoption of a siege mentality vis-à-vis the residents. Since this facility specialized in the treatment of criminal offenders, one might imagine that the siege mentality came from a fear of the residents. All the residents had some kind of criminal record, many had served time in prison, and some had committed violent crimes, including murder. However, throughout the twenty-six months I spent at DTF, I never feared for my physical safety. The siege mentality among counselors, the establishment of 'us and them' categories, originated in a different kind of anxiety, whose nature did not become clear to me until later.

Initially, much of my energy was directed at learning the routine and merely copying, without question, the way other counselors carried out their jobs. To learn the job, I 'became' a counselor in that I did not just learn the how and what of the position but identified with it and the other counselors. I found myself taking on the attitudes of the other counselors, hanging out with them in an office with the door closed against the residents, and always seeking out their company (rather than that of residents) during brief periods of free time in the work day. In sum, I became a comrade with the counselors, and consequently the residents became 'others' to me.

Some of this identification with the other counselors was self-conscious and intentional; it was part of my strategy of learning the job and part of my research strategy of participant-observation. I discovered that the siege mentality came from viewing the residents as corrupt and potentially corrupting; hence, one had to keep a distance in order to avoid becoming corrupted by their values and lifestyle.

I discovered, too, that the siege mentality and the distinct division between residents and counselors was not really a matter of choice for me. The counseling staff, including the director, looked askance at my attempts to bridge the gap. I was considered too lenient with the residents, and this imputed leniency was construed as a sign that I was being corrupted. I was 'scolded' with increasing frequency in much the same way as residents.

Especially during the last six months of my time in the facility, I was excluded from discussions of decisions that affected the residents. My source of information about what was going on shifted more toward resident scuttlebutt. While it was impossible to regard me as a resident, neither was I viewed as part of the inner circle of counselors.

At the same time that I was being excluded from the confidence of counselors, I was included more by residents. Again, this was not because they saw me as one of them, but rather because they considered me to be a different kind of counselor, perhaps one who was less concerned about discipline and more interested in their problems.

My own identification had shifted toward the residents within my first year at the facility. Frankly, I found the residents more interesting than the staff. I spent more time 'doing therapy' and much less time chatting with my coworkers.

Moreover, my dual role as counselor and researcher had become increasingly untenable. At the beginning of the project I had considered possible conflicts between the two roles. I believed then and still hold that ethnographic research and psychotherapy are not only compatible but are two sides of the same coin. In both cases the goal is to investigate, analyze, and interpret. What the patient (in the case of therapy) or the research subjects do with the information is up to them. However, as a counselor at DTF, I was expected to tell people how they should live their lives, and, to me, that seems incompatible with both research and therapy.

After my departure from DTF, I was able to maintain communications with about two dozen people who had been residents. This allowed me to fill in a good deal of the residents' point of view in a situation where they no longer had to worry about the threat of punishment or of being sent back to jail for something they might tell me. In addition, I was able to interview a number of counselors, some of whom were still employed at DTF and some of whom had left before or shortly after my arrival. These interviews, too, were extremely helpful in giving me a more complete picture of the establishment.

Three years passed before I felt able to make sufficient sense of the place to write this ethnography. Even so, I can only represent a small slice of the real-life complexities of the social scene at DTF. Moreover, my continued contact with some of the staff there suggests that significant changes have taken place in some of the particulars, especially in that counselors enjoy a more professional status and a higher pay scale than when I was there.

THE CASE STUDY

This is a case study of one residential therapeutic community for drug-abuse treatment. Data for the study were obtained primarily through my participant-observation in one residential drug treatment facility (DTF) from April 1984 to July 1986.

Therapeutic communities have not been studied very much using participant-observation, unlike, for instance, mental hospitals, which became a favorite kind of locale for the methodology. Therapeutic communities tend not to be accessible to social scientists. My access to DTF came about only because I was employed there as a counselor. Although I went into the situation with the intention of studying it, and informed the staff, the director, and the administrator of my intent, they were never especially interested in the research and generally forgot that I was doing it. The residents were much more interested in the idea that I would be writing about the place, because they wanted their story to be told.

From the point of view of both staff and residents, I was always primarily a counselor. Most of the time, I felt this way as well, because I needed the salary. However, the sense of distance experienced by participant-observer researchers was compounded in my case, because at the same time I was involved in psychoanalytic training. That is, I was engaged in my personal analysis and case supervision, using my cases at DTF for supervision purposes. In effect, this meant a sort of double research program, because psychoanalysis, at least in my training, is first a research tool and only secondarily, in fact serendipitously, a therapeutic tool. The psychoanalytic perspective, stemming from Freud's warning against "therapeutic ambition," is probably antithetical to drug treatment as a whole, and certainly antithetical to the kind of treatment that occurs at DTF.

Another intellectual interest contributed to both aspects of my participant-observation: the methodology of 'ethnography of speaking' (Hymes, 1962, 1964). This methodology considers talk as its focus of study. It is not only compatible with but an intrinsic part of both psychoanalysis and ethnographic research.

These three analytic frameworks were brought together with my counselor functions in what was for me a dramatic way. One of the residents for whom I was "primary therapist" asked for a book about the psychology of drug addiction. The book I loaned her was *The Hidden Dimension* by Leon Wurmser (1978), which offers a psychoanalytic viewpoint, but more importantly contains a wealth of case material, which I thought this resident would find interesting. She did indeed find it interesting, so much so that she persuaded me to offer a 'class' built around the book to the residents. I distributed photocopies of relevant passages to the residents in the 'class.'

In his book, Wurmser uses a goodly amount of psycho-analytic jargon, which I had to explain to the residents so that they could follow his arguments. It was not too long before I found myself having to explain the concept of re-pression in a form to which the residents could relate their own experiences. I thought I had hit upon a perfect exam-ple. Many of the residents in the 'class' had been on the publicly operated methadone program at one time or an-other, and they often complained of its corrupt, intimidat-ing, and controlling practices. I pointed out to them how difficult it would be for them to make this information pub-lic. They would probably encounter massive obstacles, in-cluding reprisals, and in the end, despite their efforts, their information would be repressed. At the time, I was trying to convey the systematic nature of repression. In fact, as a ped-agogical device, this example did prove to be effective, but it also proved effective for my understanding of DTF and my position in it as a counselor.

I had been conducting my one-on-one sessions with resi-dents according to the psychoanalytic principle of asking them to say whatever occurred to them. My job in this en-terprise was to help insure the free flow of talk. I had to identify blockages to it, and then say something to help overcome the interruption. In a more typical psycho-therapeutic situation these blockages (or "resistances") often stem from a combination of the intrapsychic conflicts of the patient and the state of the transference; in the situation here, the most common source of resistance usually had its source in institutional factors. I found that residents were restrained in their talk to me because they believed that any-thing they said could and would be used against them.

At the same time, I began to notice that it was not just 'confessional' kinds of talk that were restrained. All kinds of things were never mentioned or were discussed in some par-ticular circumstances, but not in others. The picture that began to emerge looked very much like repression, but on an institu-tionalized, social scale rather than on an intrapsychic scale.

For example, sex and race were never discussed in therapy groups. It is not that sex was never mentioned; but the only reference was to violations of rules that regulated residents' sexual conduct. In one of the first therapy groups I conducted as a counselor, one resident talked about becoming a father, another talked about her boyfriend, a third talked about feeling "cooped up," about lacking intimate relationships. No one referred to sex. One would have thought the first resident's paternity had to do with a stork and that the second's "boyfriend" was a gradeschool date. Such reluctance to talk about sexuality could be attributed to general social inhibition, except that such inhibitions disappear when the issue is a rule violation.

While I was still busy rationalizing, I attempted to 'correct' this by introducing the topics myself. My belief was that residents did not discuss these issues because of unrealistic fears based on general, social inhibitions. Such fears, I told myself, were unrealistic because *inside* the facility "openness and honesty" were encouraged and protected. Unfortunately, when the residents did begin to talk about sex and race more openly, some residents were put on "communication bans," and others had their views ridiculed or used as explanations for lack of "progress in treatment," about which their probation officers were kept well informed.

These reprisals were heavily disguised and rationalized by the counselors who imposed them so as to mask the connections between the punishments and talk about sex and race. The counselors would justify these reprisals by reference to other "problems" such as "inappropriate" attitudes, a sudden "lack of progress," or specific rule violations that until that point had been overlooked. Why this elision of the connections between the punishments and the talk? I concluded that what was being concealed from residents and counselors alike was that a primary function of counselors in DTF is to keep a lid on sexual and racial tensions.

What is true for issues of sex and race is even more true for drug abuse. As a counselor, I found that I could breach the repressions surrounding sex and race on an individual and interpersonal basis with residents, as long as I kept such communication confined to the individual sessions. I could talk with residents about my identity as a white male and what that meant to them, but I could not discuss systematic repression without putting the residents at risk for punishments from the treatment system. I was totally powerless when it came to the matter of drug abuse. Concerning this issue, counselors exist to keep a lid on the way the drug market operates and to make sure drug users stay in their places in the drug market. There was certainly no place for the notion that the residents are the victims of drug abuse rather than the abusers—those people who profit from the phenomenon.

My original intent was to study the patterns of communication and interaction among participants. Ideally, such an approach would employ mechanical recording using audio and/or video tapes. However, several attempts to use audio recordings led me to abandon this technique because it was too intrusive and disruptive. Residents of the facility were constrained in their talk in the presence of recording equipment because they feared that such a record could be used as evidence against them in the treatment program and in a court of law. (Many residents faced criminal prosecution or were under correctional supervision.) Therefore, I relied on notes written after I had left the facility each day.

In addition to data gathered through participant-observation in the facility, I interviewed the program director and several employees of the administering agency to obtain historical information. I was also able to interview probation officers who regularly referred their probationers to this treatment program.

Since I left the job, I have maintained contact with some former residents and have continued to gather interview data from them. In addition, I have reviewed public documents kept by the government agency that funds this and other drug treatment programs in the county, and I have interviewed functionaries in that agency.

I also have observed other drug treatment facilities, although far less intensively and less formally than DTF. These have included a residential facility for women, a medically oriented residential facility, and several "half-way" houses that provide residential supervision, but not "treatment." In addition, I have interviewed counselors who work in a variety of drug treatment settings, including outpatient counseling clinics, inpatient hospital units, and a drug treatment unit in a Veterans' Administration facility.

DESCRIPTION OF THE FACILITY

DTF is a single, free-standing facility located in a large midwestern city. It is mandated by the county and state governments to provide residential drug-abuse treatment for adults. It is licensed by a state regulatory agency that oversees all residential facilities for adults. Most of its operating revenue comes from a county government agency, which disperses funds originating at the federal, state, and local levels of government.

Almost all residents are recruited through the criminal justice system, but no one is sentenced, placed by the courts, or admitted through civil commitment. A majority of residents (approximately two-thirds) are on probation or parole, and many of them enter the institution as an alternative to revocation of their probation or parole. This two-thirds estimate is based on sources of referral. That is, two-thirds of admissions are referred by probation officers. However, since many residents enter at some point in criminal proceedings against them, many of those who are not on probation at the time of admission are put on probation sometime during their residency. Almost all of the remainder are awaiting trial or sentencing on criminal charges. Admission is formally voluntary and the facility is not locked.

The capacity of the facility is twenty-seven people, but the average census is twenty-four. There are three kinds of resident bedrooms, containing one, two, or three beds. The facility also contains a kitchen, dining areas, common rooms, and staff offices.

A private, non-profit social service agency administers the facility. This agency also administers a number of other facilities and programs aimed at criminal offenders. Although the treatment program has a consulting physician, it should not be thought of as operating under medical authority, nor is there any medical treatment in the strict sense of that term; that is, there are no interventions requiring medical licensure.

The total number of admissions for the years 1984 and 1985 was 232. This period overlaps with my period of field observation from April 1984 through June 1986. At any one time, somewhat less than half of the residents were black (101 by my count of the total for the period). During the observation period, ten residents identified themselves as Hispanic, and one as Native American. The remainder were white. Women consituted 15 percent (35 out of 232) of all admissions, but the number of women in the facility at one time never exceeded six, and there were periods of several months' duration when there was no woman or only one in the facility.

Confession of drug abuse is a necessary criterion for admission. For the most part, residents identify themselves as abusers of illicit drugs (heroin, cocaine, marijuana, etc.) or abusers of ethical drugs (benzodiazepines, barbituates, synthetic opiates, etc.). A few residents say they abuse alcohol but not other drugs. However, relatively few are self-identified alcoholics because such persons tend to be routed to other treatment programs. Nonetheless, the rules of this facility do not preclude admitting alcohol abusers.

The staff has several kinds of positions. Including the program director, there are four counselors; they are responsible for all therapeutic direction. Counselor positions are paraprofessional in that there is no particular criterion of professional competency. House managers provide facility supervision overnight and on weekends when counselors are not in the facility. House managers have no therapeutic responsibility. Usually there is only one house manager on duty at a time. Ancillary staff consists of a consulting physician, a consulting psychologist, a part-time dietitian, and a part-time occupational therapist or art therapist. During the fieldwork period, there were a number of counselor interns who worked in the institution as part of their clinical training in counseling related programs at several schools and universities.

HISTORY OF THE INSTITUTION

The agency that administers the facility purchased it in 1979. The institution was first established in 1973 as a private, non-profit foundation. It was organized by a former member of Synanon, who replicated that program. At first, fiscal support was based on contributions solicited from the community and earnings gained by members of the program from extra-institutional employment. During the final years of this regime, income was supplemented by a "purchase-of-service" contract with a county funding agency. A number of "treatment slots" were supported by public monies via this "purchase-of-service" contract. The foundation that ran the program had turned to public funding reluctantly, but it was forced to do so because other sources of revenue were insufficient to maintain the facility.

Even after the foundation accepted government funds, the fiscal basis was not sound because funded "treatment slots" were often vacant. As part of the philosophy of Synanon-style therapeutic communities, persons seeking admission were expected to prove their commitment to the communal endeavor. This proof often consisted of waiting in the facility for up to several days before anyone would recognize their presence, let alone formally admit them. Thereafter, new residents were typically subjected to an intensive form of hazing resembling the kind found in some military academies (see Yablonsky, 1965). One result of these policies was that the census of the institution remained well below capacity. When the current administering agency purchased the program and the physical plant in 1979, it put an end to the proof of commitment policy and reduced harassment of new residents.

While changes in internal policy were important in raising the census, external recruitment policies were perhaps even more significant. Under the old regime, an informal criterion for admission was addiction to heroin; after 1979, abuse of any drugs became a sufficient criterion. Moreover, linkages to the criminal justice system were fostered, especially to the state department of probation and parole, so that an increasing number of referrals came from probation officers. As a result, the average census was close to capacity; in fact, during my field observation, there was a substantial waiting list for admission.

From the point of view of participants in the institution, the most dramatic changes made by the agency after 1979 were alterations in the social organization within the program. In the traditional Synanon style therapeutic community, staff members and residents formed a continuum of statuses. Staff members were, in effect, a resident elite composed of those who were most senior in the program. Not all staff members emerged from the residents of this particular therapeutic community; some, like the director, came from other, similar institutions. However, residents could see something like a career ladder that, in theory, was entirely internal to the therapeutic community. Not only did staff members emerge from the resident population, but they also resided in the institution. In keeping with the continuum model, staff members were always liable to demotion back to even the lowest rank of resident status.

After the current administration purchased the program, staff members no longer resided in the facility, and most of the previous staff were replaced by paraprofessionals, who did not necessarily come from other therapeutic communities. One of the old staff members remained, and he became the program director under the new administration. The new staff members owed their position to their status as employees of the agency, not to the internal social order of the therapeutic community.

Concomitant with this dichotomization of residents and staff was a change in the position of residents, because their length of stay in the institution came under the control of the county funding source, an agency of government. This change reflected a different viewpoint regarding the function of the institution. In traditional therapeutic communities, "the goal of treatment is a global change in the individual through an integration of conduct, feelings, values, and attitudes associated with a socially drug-free life-style. . . . Its social organization is a family surrogate system, vertically stratified" (DeLeon, 1985: 825).

In the government coopted facility, global change in the individual remains the stated therapeutic goal. However, a resident of the traditional therapeutic community was expected to be committed to the communal movement and lifestyle even after leaving the institution; no such commitment is intended or even desired under the present program. Currently, residents are expected to enter the institution for a limited time for treatment and rehabilitation so that upon completion of the program they can return to the larger society with more conventional ways of life. The difference in functions is reflected by the intensive case reviews conducted of any residents who remain in the institution for longer than nine months. In other words, continued residency must be justified according to therapeutic criteria.

CHAPTER 2

The Residents

THE MOST EFFECTIVE PATH to admission into DTF is to get into trouble with the law. DTF relies on referral-driven recruitment. Procedures for entering this facility depend on referral from a third party. In keeping with this system, individuals who seek admission on their own are called "self-referrals." While many drug treatment programs rely on this method of recruitment, most receive the bulk of their referrals from other treatment programs, social service agencies, private practitioners (physicians, psychologists, etc.), and/or employee assistance programs. In contrast, DTF receives almost all of its referrals from some segment of the criminal justice system.

The principal referral sources are probation and parole officers (this source accounts for an estimated 60 percent of all referrals),[1] bail monitors who work in a different sector of the service agency of which DTF is a part,[2] and the public defender's office. Referrals from other sources rarely result in an admission, because such inquiries are discouraged through the admissions procedures: phone calls are not returned or their return is tardy, paperwork is neglected or lost, and typically, even if the referral source perseveres, the admission date is set so far in advance that the referred client never reports. During the twenty-six months of my field research, only two individuals entered the program as a result of referrals from outside the criminal justice system, and no "self-referrals" were admitted. The reasons for this informal discrimination will be examined in the next chapter; suffice it to say at this point that almost all people admitted to DTF have some kind of criminal or legal constraint.

Not only do most referrals come from the criminal justice system, but almost all people who are admitted come directly from jail. Either they are in jail because of a criminal proceeding or they are in jail pending revocation of their probation or parole. In the first case, their admission to DTF is a condition of bail; in the second case, it is an alternative to probation/parole revocation. Therefore, a virtual prerequisite for admission to DTF is incarceration.

The other requirement for admission is a confession of addiction to illicit drugs. Both 'addiction' and 'illicit' have rather special meanings. Prospective residents are deemed to be addicted if their use of drugs is "more than occasional," "causes problems in their lives," and/or is directly related to their criminal status. According to these criteria, one can be "addicted" to drugs that usually are not considered to have addictive properties—that is, marijuana. Drugs that are illegal to possess, such as heroin or cocaine, are of course "illicit," but so are drugs that are obtained through fraudulent use of prescriptions. Confession to alcoholism can result in admission, but most people who admit to "excessive" drinking are referred to treatment programs that specialize in alcoholism.

Many residents know about the program before entering DTF. Prospective residents may obtain information from more or less official sources as well as some less formal sources. Some residents receive a pre-admission interview with a DTF staff member while they are in jail. Others are told about DTF by a bail monitor, their probation/parole agent, or their public defender. In addition, the program is rather well known "on the street," so that information can be gleaned from people who were residents in the past.

Based on this prior information, most residents recall forming an image of DTF as highly restrictive and punitive. Despite this rather gloomy picture, they opt to enter the treatment program "voluntarily" as an alternative to remaining in jail.

Having agreed to enter DTF, prospective residents are placed on a waiting list. The wait can be as short as three days or as long as three months. Three days is a minimum because all residents must be approved for admission by the funding agency. This is almost always a *pro forma* process involving the transfer of a document that certifies approval. However, the wait can extend for months depending on the vagaries of the criminal process—for example, a bail hearing—procedures followed by the office of probation and parole, the availability of space in the facility on a particular day, and other unpredictable circumstances. Since the prospective resident usually is in jail, the wait is administratively inconsequential; the resident is not going anywhere. In any case, there are no "emergency" admissions.

Once the day of admission arrives, the soon-to-be resident must get from jail to DTF. Occasionally individuals are discharged from incarceration and allowed to report on their own. More commonly, a bail monitor, a probation agent, or some other functionary transports them. Unless this transportation includes a stop at the home of the resident—it usually does not—new residents arrive at the facility with only the clothing on their backs and a small plastic bag of valuables obtained from the jail's property room. Procuring additional clothing and their other personal possessions is immediately problematic, because of the restrictions imposed on new arrivals. They need special permission from a staff member in order to contact anyone outside the facility who is not a criminal justice functionary, and this limitation includes telephone calls.

GETTING INTO TREATMENT

The entry door is locked and must be opened from the inside. The facility has a small foyer at its front entrance. On the wall to the right is a hand-lettered sign that informs the entrant of the four "cardinal rules":

1. No drugs in or on your person
2. No violence or threats of violence
3. No sexual contact or romantic behavior
4. All information is to be kept confidential

New residents are told that they must see a counselor before they can be admitted, and so begins the "intake" process. This initial "intake" interview is always conducted by one of the counseling staff members, and the new resident's probation/parole officer or a bail monitor occasionally is present. On the other hand, new residents are often just dropped off at the facility by whoever brought them. During this interview, the resident must sign a number of documents: an "admission agreement/consent to treatment," a "client rights/complaint procedure," a disclaimer of program responsibility for personal property, a waiver of the right to confidentiality of treatment, a waiver of confidentiality to the funding agency, and a waiver of confidentiality to the state department of corrections. In addition to these signatory documents, counselors who conduct "intake" interviews fill out a number of forms based on their interrogation of new arrivals. One of these is the "face sheet," which includes some demographic information, legal status (probation/parole, pending court appearances, criminal charges, etc.), educational attainment, number of dependents, emergency contacts, and a brief drug-use history. The counselor also fills out a "significant other" form that includes a section calling for the name of the resident's probation/parole officer, the date and nature of the next court appearance, the name of the judge, and the name of the defense attorney. Finally there is a form that consists of a very short "mental health" questionnaire including questions about hallucinations, suicidal thoughts, feelings of depression, and anxiety. On the same form is a section for assignment to a resident work crew. The counselor might or might not assign the inductee to a "primary therapist" (usually not), and assignment to a therapist can take up to a week.

After the interview with the counselor, new residents are turned over to a resident who has gained seniority in the program, someone who has been in residence for at least three or four months. The senior resident gives a tour of the facility, makes introductions, describes the rules of the program, and provides general orientation.

The facility is a converted apartment building, three stories high, built in the 1920s. It is in an older, working-class residential neighborhood with probably the greatest degree of racial-ethnic heterogeneity in this otherwise highly segregated city. On the ground floor of the building are the common rooms—the kitchen, dining areas, TV room, and so on. When residents are on the ground floor, they are "on the floor." The two upper stories contain the bedrooms, some staff offices, and a general purpose room. Part of the basement is finished so that it can be used for large group meetings, and it also has a pool table and some other recreational equipment.

Sometime during their first day, new residents are assigned a bed, typically in one of the rooms shared with two others. Any personal belongings they have brought are searched, either by a staff member or a senior resident, before the new residents are allowed to put them in their bedrooms under supervision. They then must return to "the floor," the common-room areas on the ground floor; they cannot return to their bedrooms until bedtime (11:00 PM) except with supervision, and then only with permission from a counselor.

After signing a flurry of documents, being introduced to twenty or so strangers by first name, listening to a thirty- or forty-five-minute recitation of about two hundred rules, shuffling off to a bedroom already occupied by two other unknown persons, giving a urine sample under supervision, then perhaps hanging out in the TV room with a few other relatively new entrants, all this having just left jail and maybe facing continued felony prosecutions, the new arrival is expected to act "appropriately" (i.e., according to the rules) with a group of drug addicts and shadowy staff persons, who seem to notice only those new residents who are acting "negatively" (i.e., against the rules).

For most new residents, the "street" reputation of the program adds to their confusion. This reputation centers on such practices as making residents wear demeaning signs or regalia such as dunce caps or diapers, being forced to scrub floors with toothbrushes, or having one's head shaved. While such occurrences were not uncommon ten years ago, these kinds of practices are not now part of the treatment program, although the reputation lingers.

Who's Who

Getting to know 'who is who' is important in any social situation, since the positions of those with whom one interacts are important determinants in shaping appropriate and effective conduct. In DTF the formal social structure is made quite explicit, and it is learned quickly and easily by new residents. Of course, there are informally structured social arrangements, but they are far less powerful and significant for reasons that will be explored later. It is the formal structure that is of immediate concern to new arrivals.

The sharpest division of the social structure separates residents from staff members. Residents live here and are the objects of various services provided by staff members. Staff members work here, but live elsewhere, and their occupational tasks are directed at the residents.

The residents' interaction with regular staff (counselors and house managers) is continuous and daily, while their interaction with auxiliary staff like the consulting psychologist and physician takes place only occasionally or not at all. For counselors and house managers, the structure is more or less hierarchical. The program director is also a counselor; he tells other counselors and house managers what to do. Counselors can tell house managers what to do, but not vice versa, and counselors can act as house managers, but house managers cannot take on the obligations of counselors. Knowledge of these authority relationships among staff members is crucial for residents because they need to know who can do what to them and for them.

New arrivals must find out where they stand in the resident hierarchy as well. There are two formal structures, one for work crews and another that pertains to overall status in the program. There are four crews, or "departments" as they are called: kitchen, maintenance, communications, and laundry. Each crew has a chief and an assistant. The chiefs or department heads plan work and assign tasks to the crew members. Participation in work is daily, so that by the day after admission, new residents are working under the supervision of a department head. Other than the department heads and assistants, there is no persistent authority structure to the work crews unless the work is task-specific; one resident may have more skill with respect to a particular task and therefore may direct the work of others.

The other formal hierarchy among residents is the structure of their overall status in the program. There are three components to this structure, which represent phases based on length of residency or seniority and a more nebulous criterion known as "progress." These two criteria overlap, but they are not entirely co-extensive. The phases or resident status categories are initial assessment (IA), intermediate program (IP), and graduation program (GP). From the residents' point of view, these three categories represent increasing degrees of freedom.

The IA category is the most restrictive, and all new residents are placed in it automatically. A new resident remains in this category usually for no less than three weeks up to no more than six weeks, although there is no hard and fast rule about how long a resident may be in IA. While in this category, residents are not allowed to leave the building or even go "off the floor" (leave the ground floor common rooms) without supervision and permission from a staff member. IA residents are not allowed to make phone calls, have visits, or drink any beverages other than water except at mealtimes, unless they have special permission from a counselor. Two rationales are given to residents for the highly restrictive conditions. Residents should be separating themselves from their "dope fiend" lifestyles and learning about the treatment program. In addition, the IA category is supposed to be a period in which the resident, in conjunction with the resident's assigned "primary therapist," assesses what is needed for rehabilitation. In keeping with the purpose of assessment, this period should be relatively free from disruptions and responsibilities, and it should provide a neutral time or baseline for a diagnostic behavioral evaluation. Hence, contact outside the facility is severely limited, as are "privileges," or freedoms and responsibilities.

In practice, residents in IA are required to participate in a number of activities that contradict both of these rationales. They are given a general physical examination performed at a clinic outside DTF. They take at least one psychological test;[3] sometimes several are administered. The resident may be interviewed by the consulting psychologist as well. Unless the resident has a high-school diploma or its equivalent, s/he takes some educational assessment tests. The assessment phase of the program is the period during which most residents have the most business with the criminal justice system. Court appearances, meetings with attorneys, meetings with probation officers, and the like are more frequent than at any other period of residency. In fact, IA residents may participate in more extra-facility business than IP residents. What is more restricted for residents in assessment is contact with friends and family members.

The second category includes residents who are in the intermediate program (IP). Residents in this category can gain greater freedom by earning "privileges," which in effect remove the civil disabilities under which IA residents must labor. Therefore, it is important to move out of the IA category and into IP. This is accomplished by completing assessment. Completing assessment includes a few objective criteria,[4] but far more important is demonstrating that one has achieved "stability in the program." Of course "stability" is a subjective and global criterion, but the following is a list of signs of "instability":

1. Habitual breaking of a specific rule or group of rules.

2. Back stabbing—complaining or talking about someone behind their back.

3. War stories—discussion between residents about drugs or glorifying their drug-using lifestyle.

4. Laziness in doing your job, in group sessions, or any other part of the program.

5. Sloppiness—not attending to the cleanliness of your area or yourself.

6. Lying to any other person.

7. Bickering—arguing with other people over unnecessary things.

8. Complaining.

9. Not following directions of another resident, council member, department head, or staff member.

10. Manipulation—using devious or dishonest means to gain or achieve something which could have been or should not have been gained through honest and open behavior.

11. Sarcasm.

12. Negative contract—agreement between residents to allow or ignore something negative.

13. Not following the schedule.

14. Mother loving—doing things for other people they could have done themselves.

15. Reacting or copping attitudes towards other residents or staff—other belligerent behavior.

16. Taking materials from a department without permission.

17. Sleeping during scheduled activities.

18. Abuse of any procedure or rule which establishes or limits behavior.

19. Intimidation: directly or indirectly threatening another resident.

20. Refusal to become involved in program activities.

21. Misuse of leadership position.

22. Misuse of program property. Any additional suspicious or problem-creating activity.

23. Profanity: Habitual and consistent use of undesirable language.

The foregoing list of signs of "instability" is given to residents in writing. A comment at the end of the list notes, "Continual difficulties in above areas may result in the group [of residents] and/or staff requesting that the persons involved abide by special limitations, restrictions, or learning activities to reduce or improve the difficulty." While not exhaustive, these criteria or signs suggest the general framework for understanding what "stability" means and what "progress in treatment" means. The list can be conceived as the outline for the moral economy of the program: residents who abide by these guidelines increase their moral accounts and make progress toward successful graduation from the treatment program. Such residents are deemed to be rehabilitated.

Residents in the IA category who exhibit signs of "stability" and show "progress in treatment" are promoted into the IP category. Residents remain in the IP category longer than in any other. Having achieved IP status, they can work toward gaining "privileges," which remove some of the restrictions on their liberty. For example, they can earn the "privilege" of unmonitored telephone conversations, permission to leave the building without supervision, drinking coffee or tea outside of mealtimes, and the like.

The mechanism for earning privileges is a weekly meeting of all IP residents, held under the supervision of a staff member. During this meeting residents present personal goals toward which they intend to work during the coming week. Both the quality of the goals and the degree of attainment are evaluated by the group, who then vote to award points to each other, and the points can be redeemed for specific privileges. In the voting, a resident's overall "progress in treatment" is supposed to be part of the evaluation. Thus, if a resident establishes valued goals and attains them but fails to demonstrate overall "progress in treatment" he or she may not earn "privileges." Moreover, the counselor can modify awards either by overriding the vote or by intervening in the deliberations of the meeting to channel the vote in a particular direction. Following is a list of privileges and the number of points needed for each:

PRIVILEGES AND RATING

1. *Phone Calls* (20 points)   Eligible to make or receive thirty-minute phone calls from 8:00 AM through 10:30 PM. With Late Hours, able to make or receive phone calls during late hours (until 12:30 AM). May make unmonitored calls during regular phone hours.

2. *Late Hours* (15 points)   May remain on floor until 12:30 AM on weekdays; 2:30 AM on weekends.

3. *Twenty-Minute Walks* (10 points)   May take one walk (or jog) per day until 8:00 PM.

4. *Overnight Pass* (30 points)   May request overnight pass twice per month with counselor approval.

5. *Weekday Pass* (18 points)   May request one four-hour pass per week with counselor approval.

6. *Time-Out* (12 points)   May request from staff on duty up to three hours once per week or two two-hour periods of private relaxation off the floor per week.

7. *Snack and Store Runs* (12 points)   May purchase and eat own snacks during snack time. May make store runs for all residents during weekdays.

8. Coffee/Tea Privilege (8 points)   May purchase and drink own coffee/tea during snack time. May drink coffee/tea made by house until 3:00 PM.

9. Library Time (5 points)   May utilize library for personal study one hour per day.

10. Change of Departments (5 points)   This applies to resident changing departments in worker status only. May not be used to avoid difficulty in department.

11. Voting (5 points)   With membership this privilege establishes the new IP resident in the above process.

Because IP is the longest phase of the treatment program, at any one time the majority of residents are in this category. They are working toward the final phase of the program, which is the highest category (in the moral economy) and carries with it the least restrictive status. This category or phase is the graduation program (GP), which usually is associated with regular vocational or educational activity outside the facility. GP residents are expected to be looking for work, working, or attending school during the day. They continue to reside in the facility, and are expected to participate in the collective treatment activities as their work or school schedule permits.

The GP phase is supposed to provide residents with a controlled path toward reintegration in the community and allow them to build resources (e.g., money, housing, "positive" friends) in anticipation of their graduation or successful discharge. GP residents are not required to be in work crews. They have all the "privileges" that can be earned, but they are expected to demonstrate continued "progress in treatment." As the most senior residents, they are expected to provide moral leadership for residents in the lower categories. Relatively few residents remain in the program long enough to make it to the GP category. Usually there are only three or four GP residents, and sometimes there is none.

In addition to the work crews and the three resident categories, there is another structured apparatus known as the Council. The Council consists of one representative selected by vote from IA; two representatives from IP; and all GP members. The Council is a sort of parliament representing resident interests. It meets weekly under the supervision of a counselor. While in theory the Council has general parliamentary functions, in practice it has about as much power as did the European parliaments under the absolute monarchies. The only consistently effective actions taken by the Council are to mete out punishments against residents for rule infractions or general "negative" behavior (in the absence of specific delicts). Membership on the Council is an honor, and, especially for IA and IP residents, it is both a reward for and a sign of "progress in treatment."

THE TREATMENT DAY

Knowledge of the formal social structure among residents is essential for survival in the program. It is also essential to know what to do and how to act during the treatment day. Just as the social hierarchy is arranged in a more or less sequential fashion, where length of residency is roughly correlated with seniority, status, and freedom, so the treatment day is arranged according to a sequence of collective activities and ceremonies.

For residents in the kitchen crew who are assigned to breakfast, the day begins at about 6:00 AM so that they can serve the meal by 7:30, when all other residents must be "on the floor." As with all meals, breakfast is served family style. Before sitting at the table to eat, one resident leads the others in a prayer. This usually is rather short, and its content and style are American, non-sectarian Christian. The food is served and the tables are set by the kitchen crew, but all residents must wash their own plates when they are finished.

After breakfast, there is a "tighten-up" involving general cleaning and straightening, sweeping floors, dusting, emptying ash trays, and so on. The "tighten-up" of the common rooms and staff offices is performed by members of the maintenance crew. "Tighten-ups" of the dormitory areas are under the direction of dorm captains. Kitchen crew members wash the kitchen and clean cooking utensils, unless a resident has been assigned a "tighten-up" as a punishment. "Tighten-ups" are common punishments given by the Council, so there are often several residents who relieve the kitchen crew in this way.

Morning Meeting

Morning meeting begins promptly at 9:00 AM. Attendance is mandatory for all residents except those in GP. Although their attendance is encouraged by the staff, GP residents seldom attend, and this exemption is considered to be one of the advantages of that status. Because this is the only resident gathering where staff members are rarely in attendance, it appears to be a resident-determined activity.

The meeting begins with a recitation of "The Philosophy."

> We are here because there is no refuge finally from ourselves, until we confront ourselves in the eyes and hearts of others we are running. Until we suffer others to share in our secrets, we

have no safety from them, afraid to be known we can neither know ourselves nor any others, we will be alone, where else but in this common ground can we find such a mirror, here together we can at last appear clearly to ourselves, not as the giant of our dreams nor the dwarf of our fears, but as a human being a part of a whole with a share in its purpose. In this ground we can each take root and grow, not alone anymore as in death but alive to ourselves and others. We share in this belief that if you treat us as we are we will stay as we are, but if you treat us as we could be and should be we will become as we could be and should be because the family is a place where we arrive together we should give this place to all forever.

Mother lovers
Unconditional: Rewards good and bad behavior.
Rejecting: Rejects good and bad behavior.
Indifferent: Does not care either way.
Vacillating: All these mother lovers combined.

Motivations
Deadly: Substitutes one substance for another, such as pills for heroin!
Guilty: Feels they made him/her that way and wants to cure him/her themselves.
Impatient: Wants to take him/her out of treatment before he or she has completed the program.
Fearful: Fears that once he or she has completed the program he or she may leave them.

After the reading, each resident in turn stands and greets everyone else by saying, "Good morning, family." After this ritual greeting, the residents proclaim their individual goals for the day, which always include an assertion of remaining "drug and alcohol free"; some residents include "crime free" as well. After each resident is finished, the group responds in unison by saying, "good goals."

Next on the agenda is "in-depths." The basic format calls for a resident to go to others, stand before each one, and offer opinions about the person's character and behavior. The recipient of this "in-depth" commentary is not supposed to respond but wait until the speaker finishes and, without comment, shake the person's hand. Giving "in-depths" is rotated among residents with two members of IP and one member of IA giving them each morning. Residents give "in-depths" only to members of their own status category; that is, people in IA give them to other IAs, and those in IP give them to other IPs. There is no crossing of status categories.

The formal rationale, the one given to new residents, is that this procedure encourages open and honest expression of thoughts and feelings, unmotivated by personal relationships. This rationale is not framed as an ideal toward which one may strive, but as something that ought to be practiced all the time; the "in-depths" merely provide a formal opportunity for doing so. In practice, "in-depths" belie the name: residents tend to approach them as something to get through. Exceptions occur when someone has a particular complaint about one or several others, or when the speaker has an especially low opinion of another resident. Occasionally, then, residents will use the opportunity afforded by "in-depths" to sound off in the form of insulting epithets or subjective, emotionally laden derogations, rather than the objective evaluations that are the expected style of the "in-depths."

After "in-depths," the meeting moves on to house business: announcements, brief discussions of needed adjustments (e.g., work crew assignments), requests for bus passes, and requests for "strength." Bus passes are purchased from the program's general funds and provided to residents who have to leave the facility on approved business—for example, medical appointments, court appearances, appointments with a probation officer. "Strength" is the term used to designate either the procedure or the person who accompanies another resident in order to monitor his/her behavior while out of the facility. Individuals in IA automatically need "strength," and IP residents who are "on restriction" (those whose "privileges" have been revoked as

punishment for a rule infraction) also need "strength."
Agreeing to act as "strength" for another person is voluntary, but it is also supposed to demonstrate "responsible behavior."

The meeting ends with the "Serenity Prayer." In this ceremony, all residents join hands and recite the memorized
prayer.

> God grant me the serenity to accept the things I cannot
> change. The courage to change the things I can. And the wis-
> dom to know the difference. Amen.

The morning meeting is serious business for residents in
DTF. On the one hand, everyone is aware that the rites are
theatrical, that performances here are different from those
of 'real life,' life outside the facility. On the other hand,
much rides on their appropriate performance. Almost all the
residents face probation or parole revocation and/or sentencing for criminal offenses, and their success in treatment
here can mean the difference between prison and freedom.
Yet, this seriousness does not entirely remove a theatrical,
play-like understanding; it defers it, sets aside the play for
another time and place. The deferred, submerged, or repressed meaning of the morning meeting sometimes becomes observable and explicit.

One such occasion arose when the residents went to the
zoo as a group. This was a special trip, which broke the
daily routine. They left the facility before breakfast, so that
the meal was eaten in the zoo coffee shop. They decided to
enact the morning meeting performance as an irony, ironic
because this was one morning when it was not required.
Ironic too because they were acutely aware that the setting
was 'real life,' and because there were other patrons in the
coffee shop; in other words, there was a non-participating
audience. Although they played the performance
"straight"—that is, as if it were a regular morning meeting—they all thought it was hilarious, especially as they

were able to elicit stares from the coffee shop patrons. Inside the facility, immersed in the exigencies of daily routine, such meanings are not accessible to public articulation.

Morning Groups

On a normal day, the morning meeting ends at about 9:30 AM and it is directly followed by formal therapy groups. In keeping with the communitarian ideology and traditional practices in therapeutic communities, groups are thought to be the heart of therapy here. Groups of all sizes, in various locations in the facility, lasting for various durations, for various purposes, conducted by an ever-changing lineup of counseling staff, but never related to any recognizable theory of group process, are a constant for all residents and counselors. Some groups are relatively spontaneous in that they seem to convene in response to what is perceived as some immediate crisis. Other groups are planned but episodic, such as presentations of an educational nature on specific topics (e.g., AIDS among IV drug users), or more therapeutically oriented groups on topics such as sexual abuse in families. Groups such as these are often conducted by outsiders. In addition, there are the regularly scheduled groups. These are the most common.

On Monday mornings, following the morning meeting, there is a group that includes all the residents in the facility. Exceptions are those members of GP who must go to jobs or school and those residents in the other two categories who have necessary business outside the house. The express purpose of the Monday morning group is to discuss "problems over the weekend." Weekends are thought to be the most likely time for "problems" to arise because the counseling staff is not present, some residents leave the facility on weekend passes while others can have visitors, and the daily routine is less stringent than during the week. Not infrequently, more than one counselor participates in the Monday morning group. The agenda for this group usually is derived from notes written in a staff log by weekend house managers. Relevant notations are those that suggest "problems" such as rule infractions and "suspicious" behavior by residents, or some combination of the two.

Residents who have been spotlighted in the log are given the opportunity to bring up the relevant incidents themselves when a counselor calls for a recitation of "problems." The "problem"-oriented format of the Monday morning group can often turn this regularly scheduled group into a crisis group, so that it may turn into an all-day affair, or sometimes even extend over several days, until the "problem" is "resolved." "Resolution" typically means that guilty residents are punished or even expelled from the facility.

On Tuesday, Wednesday, and Thursday mornings, instead of full house groups, the residents are split into one IA group and one IP group. These are conducted by a counselor and attendance is mandatory for residents. The IA groups tend to have a relatively more educative format than does IP, and they are therefore more topical. For example, for several months there was an IA group that focused on "understanding emotions." IP groups are less topically structured, so they tend to give a forum for ongoing concerns of the residents in this category. The most clearly differentiated groups occur on Wednesday mornings: these are the "IA seminar" and the "IP privilege meeting."

The express purpose of the "IA seminar" is to give a staff-defined orientation to the program. It includes a review of various alternative drug treatment philosophies; perhaps not surprisingly, the therapeutic community philosophy always seems to come out superior to all others. There is also information provided about other treatment programs in the vicinity and a framework for the development of treatment plans.

The curriculum of the IA seminar never seems to proceed to completion, much like the high-school American history course that never seems to get past the Civil War. The seminar frequently gets pre-empted by crisis groups and other events. Moreover, membership in the IA category has a high turnover mainly due to the high drop-out rate—about 75 percent of all residents leave or are expelled in the first thirty days. Of those who remain, there are continual promotions out of IA and into IP.

A perennial topic for the seminar is the "life-problem areas" that are supposed to be the framework for individual treatment plans, which are one of the innovations resulting from government cooptation of the therapeutic community brand of drug treatment. In the case of DTF, the state licensing agency requires a written, individual treatment plan for each resident, and these are reviewed and inspected at regular intervals. The framework for the individual treatment plans is built around five "life-problem areas": medical, legal, emotional-psychological, educational-vocational, social, and drug-related. Residents are supposed to identify problems in each of these "areas" caused by drugs and their "dope fiend" lifestyle. Once the problems have been identified (and this is the formal purpose of the IA phase of the treatment program), residents in consultation with their "primary therapists" devise goals for improving each area and specify a means to achieve these goals. In the IA seminar, residents are taught what these life areas mean, and they are then expected to tell the group how drugs and crime have adversely affected them in each "area."

While the perennial topic for the IA seminar is the "life-problem areas," the perennial agenda for the residents is how to get out of IA. In fact, this is the implicit agenda for all IA groups, regardless of the explicit topic. It is especially noticeable in the seminar because formulation of the treatment plan is one of the objective criteria for promotion into IP status. The seminar especially is fraught with maneuverings on the part of residents and staff to define what is being talked about. When residents question and express discontent about their restrictive status, the counselor must find a way to relate such expression back to the "life-problem areas." For example, the counselor might relate a resident's eagerness to be promoted into IP as an example of neglect in identifying problems in general and health problems in particular, such that this neglect has now led the resident into needing extensive dental work. Continued insistence by a resident on talking about status issues can lead the counselor to characterize such concerns as indicating a lack of cooperation with treatment, which implies "instability in the program," which in turn implies that the resident in question needs to remain in IA to gain greater "stability." At this point, it becomes clear that continued talk about status restrictions can result in an even more prolonged period of restrictiveness.

Noteworthy is the fact that the counselor's strategy is never one of exercising raw power, but is always expressed in rational terms framed by the treatment ideology of the program. The counselor's threat, even when stated explicitly—"If you continue to complain about being restricted, I'll make sure you stay restricted even longer"—is always justified according to rationalized assumptions about "stability" and "identifying problems." It is also noteworthy that residents never question these assumptions. Typically the complainant couches protests in personal terms, but even if other residents in the group offer support, this support is in a "me too" form. The complaints are always about the *experience* of the restrictions; never do these residents question the validity of, for example, "life problems."

The theme of opposing agendas runs through IP groups; only the particulars vary. Of course in these groups the residents' goals are not to get promoted into IP status; however, the issue of restrictions is a constant theme here too. One reason for the similarity is that there are always several IP residents who are "on restriction." "Restrictions" are punishments given for particular rule violations that have been construed as serious—for example, an incident of illicit drug use. The standard length of a "restriction" is thirty days. For this period, IP residents "on restriction" are in effect demoted to IA status.

For IP residents who are not in a punishment status, restrictiveness is still an issue. The IP phase of the treatment program is the longest; residents stay in this phase for months. Those who have just entered this phase can look forward to the opportunity to earn "privileges" (freedoms), but as they gaze around the group of fellow IP members, they may see someone who has been in this category for eight months; thus, even at the beginning it can look like a very long row to hoe. For those who have already been in this phase for some time, and have perhaps gone through a thirty-day "restriction," residency in DTF can seem like a forever proposition. One of the concerns of many residents in this phase is that their legal pressures have been clarified. Either they have been sentenced (to probation) or their existing probation status has formally incorporated the condition of treatment at DTF. Therefore, their questions boil down to how long they have to stay here to satisfy their probation officers.

This fundamental question enters into talk in the therapy groups because counselors report residents' "progress in treatment" to their probation officers. Failure to demonstrate "progress" can result in a longer stay for IP residents just as lack of "stability" can result in a longer term in the IA category. The same issues dominate the concerns of residents in the last phase of the program, those in the GP category, but because they have an investment in extra-facility activities (jobs or school), and because they have more freedoms inside the facility, their concerns include securing the most favorable conditions for themselves once they leave DTF: GP residents are more aware of life after DTF.

There is no regularly scheduled group on Friday mornings, so residents are encouraged to make outside appointments for this time. Occasionally, special events are scheduled such as visits from the public health nurse or educational presentations by outside speakers. Individual sessions with "primary therapists" may be scheduled, and if nothing else, residents are required to participate in work crews.

Afternoon Activities

There are no regular groups in the afternoon, and activities are more diverse. This is the most common time to meet individually with one's "primary therapist." The afternoon is also when classes are held for high-school equivalency education. Residents who are not engaged in either of these activities are employed on their assigned work crews. Since afternoons are less rigidly scheduled, residents are encouraged to make appointments for necessary business outside the facility for this time of day. As a result, the in-house population is somewhat lower. There seems to be fewer people because residents are occupied in more individual projects and are less congregated.

Evenings

Although at least one regular group of one kind or another meets in the evenings, not all residents participate except for the House Meeting on Wednesdays. Residents who do not take part in evening groups have free time to engage in recreation, study for school, or work on program requirements. These program requirements call for a surprising amount of paperwork. For example, residents in IA are expected to write an autobiography. Residents in IP must outline a book entitled *Help Yourself to Happiness*, which is used as bibliotherapy, and they also have to formulate written goals to earn privileges. Those in the GP category often meet with their "primary therapist" in the evening if they are not participating in one of the therapy groups.

Wednesday night is reserved for the House Meeting, which all residents must attend. The business of this meeting is threefold: it is a forum to discuss matters of general concern and interest to all residents; written pass requests for the weekend are returned to residents with their disposition—approved, rejected, or modified; and the Council announces punishments for those residents who were brought to that tribunal.

The treatment day ends at 9:00 PM, since that is when all counseling staff go off duty and the night house manager takes over supervision. The period from 9:00 to 11:00 PM (bedtime) is free time for all residents. They can watch television, play cards, make phone calls, or engage in any activity that is not prohibited.

SURVIVING IN THE PROGRAM

The most important thing for all residents to learn and practice is survival in the program; at least this is the end to which residents direct most of their effort. Survival means avoiding expulsion and escaping punishments. Survival also implies that whatever circumstances forced people to enter DTF can be ameliorated. While there are tangible benefits that residents can gain while they are in DTF, these are secondary to what might be called the moral economy of treatment. This moral economy is the ideology in action; it is the framework for progress toward rehabilitation with its own criteria for success and failure. Surviving the program is a matter of success in the moral economy.

The moral economy should be understood as distinct from any kind of material economy or tangible benefits. It is important for new residents to learn this distinction quickly and not confuse material survival with survival in the program. DTF is presented, and for the most part functions, as a provider and protector of residents' physical and material well-being. Residents are provided with the necessities for living either by the program directly or indirectly by referral. The immediate needs of food and shelter are part of the very definition of DTF as a residential facility. Individuals without clothing can obtain some from a supply made up of items left behind by former residents. In addition, they are referred to charity clothing centers for which they can qualify by their resident status in DTF. Residents are referred regularly for free medical and dental care to the county hospital system without stigmatization: although medical or dental appointments do not in themselves arouse suspicion, the activities of residents while outside the facility or the possibility of receiving prescriptions for narcotics do arouse suspicion. The only material want not supplied by DTF is cigarettes, although this commodity had been supplied in the past and would still be supplied were it not for a combination of budget restrictions and moral objections raised by the advisory board of directors. In sum, material survival is assured; it is moral survival that is the issue.

The moral economy is based on dividing conduct into positive and negative. Actions, incidents, and attitudes come under scrutiny according to this dichotomy. The most minute occurrences are subject to this dichotomized evaluation, which means that the residents are almost always 'on-stage,' or open to evaluation by fellow residents as well as staff members. These observations then affect the moral accounts of residents. Those that are positive swell them and result in "progress in treatment," while those that are negative diminish them and put residents at risk for punishments or even expulsion.

The principal locus for the market of the moral economy is the groups, the regularly scheduled groups and perhaps even more critically the crisis groups. Groups are where residents can most effectively demonstrate that they are making "progress in treatment," and they do so by following strategies that increase their moral accounts. At the same time, residents must attend to their behavior outside of groups, because it is the extra-group goings-on that provide the topical focus of group discussions.

One of the main sources for topics of group discussion is the log in which counselors and house managers enter observations of residents and their conduct based on twenty-four hour surveillance. As mentioned in regard to the Monday morning group, log notations connoting "problems" are examined in detail for the purpose of reaching an evaluation of residents' conduct. Most often, the notes are inconclusive,

so that the group process is necessary for a definitive deter-
mination of positivity or negativity. But the log notation is
the starting point for this process; hence, knowledge of what
is in the log gives a resident a distinct advantage in the
group performance.

One strategy for gaining intelligence about the log contents depends on having a friendly relationship with one of
the staff members. Trading on the relationship, a resident
can inquire about log notations in the hope of gaining
knowledge of what the staff will be looking for in the group.
Without this knowledge, residents run the risk of confessing
to incidents that would be unknown if they had remained
quiet. An alternative strategy is to stand pat during the
group—that is, maintain silence about their own perhaps
questionable activities unless a staff member or fellow resident brings up some transgression. However, this strategy
incurs an additional risk of an accusation of not being
"open and honest" or of denying "problems" once some
delict is brought to light.

In many respects, reliance on fellow residents is the least
rewarding strategy. Other residents' knowledge of activities
in the facility is on the whole far more complete than that of
the staff, but no one knows everything that transpires, and
occasionally a staff member will know something that no-
body else knows. Fellow residents are not necessarily in a
better position than one another to know what is in the log,
unless someone has gained surreptitious access to it. The difficulty with such a source of information is that the act of
obtaining it is itself a transgression, so it behooves the one
who garnered the information to keep it as secret as possible. Perhaps the most important reason for not relying on
other residents is that doing so is construed as a "negative
contract" according to the express rules of the program.

The notion of "negative contracts" is central to the
workings of the moral economy. "Negative contracts" are
defined by the written rules of the program as including any
agreement between residents to help each other by means or

for ends that are not "positive." Both means and ends are subject to a "negative-positive" test. Many minor rules are instances of this general principle. For example, there is a rule that prohibits giving or receiving a cigarette, a rule extended to asking for, or offering, one. The rationale for this particular rule is that "owing" another resident cigarettes could incline one to overlook more serious wrongdoing.

If a third resident even observes two others in a cigarette transaction, the third resident is presumptively involved in a "negative contract"; the third resident is presumed to have 'guilty knowledge.' The second rationale entailed by the prohibition of "negative contracts" is that they are supposed to operate against the "street code" that prohibits "snitching." Breaking down the assumed value system attributed to "the street" and the "dope fiend" way of life is one of the objectives of the program. It is assumed that a code against "snitching" is an integral part of "the street" value system, hence the enormous emphasis put on "negative contracts."

Because snitching is rewarded by praise and increases one's moral account, residents can use it as a maneuver to get revenge or gain social advantage with impunity, especially since any signs of retaliation are subject to negative sanctions enforced by the staff, ranging from verbal rebuke, to public humiliation, even to expulsion from the program. Therefore, if a resident goes into, say, the Monday morning group with knowledge of someone else's "problems," he or she is presumed to have guilty knowledge, unless it is divulged at the earliest opportunity. "Problems" are defined so broadly that sometimes it is difficult to decide whether something is a "problem." They certainly include rule violations, but they *can*, although not necessarily, include physical illness or some emotional distress. Of course, "problems" vary in degree of severity, so that those that will become the focus of a group discussion go through a process of selection. An important survival skill is the ability to judge which weekend or overnight occurrences are most likely to be brought up in the group. Residents have to base this judgment on a number of factors, including: what is the prima facie severity according to program rules; which residents were involved in the incident (the more "positive" the current reputation of the implicated residents, the less likely it will be the focus of the group); which counselors are present; and what their particular bugbears are at the time. Certain "problems" always take precedence; they act as a kind of trump for the group process. The most formidable is anything pertaining to drugs, and a close second is any activity suggesting sex.

These two issues can be relied upon to dominate any group; however, there are some risks entailed in introducing these topics. Since the two major benefits of "snitching" or bringing up other residents' problems are revenge and improving one's status as a "positive" resident, one must be as Caesar's wife with respect to the incidents one chooses to introduce. On the other hand, if a resident is tangentially implicated, he or she can reduce the consequent punishment by being the first to bring up the issue and, also very important, by giving the most complete account of it. Direct knowledge of drugs or sex usually is too hot to wait through a weekend or even a night for the next day's group: there is always the risk that possessing the knowledge will backfire, and the person who knows will be accused of having "negative contracts." The risk of backfire is illustrated by the following situation.

One Saturday, Sheryl, a resident who had been in the facility for only two weeks, received an approved visitor.[5] The visitor offered her some marijuana, which she turned down. Another resident, John, had observed the offer. He approached Sheryl's visitor while she was absent for a brief period and purchased the marijuana. The visitor told Sheryl about the transaction. That evening, John offered some of the marijuana to his roommate, Bob, who also turned it down. Indecisive about what to do with the drug, John spoke with Bob about it for several hours. In exasperation with John's dithering, Bob finally told John to go and smoke it, and John proceeded to do so.

The next morning, Sunday, Sheryl told Jeff about the transaction between her visitor and John. At that time, Sheryl knew nothing of what had transpired between John and Bob the night before. Jeff was one of the more senior residents, a crew chief, and was soon scheduled to be promoted to the GP category; he was reputed to be an especially "positive" resident. Jeff was attracted to Sheryl, although the attraction was not reciprocated, but Sheryl knew of Jeff's crush on her. As a senior, "responsible," and "positive" resident, Jeff took it upon himself to cull a small group of other, "positive" residents to form an impromptu gathering consisting of Sheryl, John, Bob, himself, and two others. Jeff and the other two "positive" residents urged John and Sheryl to report the incident to the counseling staff when they returned to the facility on Monday morning.

Unfortunately, the weekend house manager "discovered" the group while it was in progress and noted it in the log. The house manager did not participate in the group or observe it for any length of time. There was no explicit rule violation in the gathering itself, so the house manager let it continue. However, the log notation characterized the group as suspicious and implied some sort of conspiracy. Therefore, by Monday morning, all the participants had been cast in a guilty light.

Imputations of Jeff's wrongdoing were predicated on his attraction to Sheryl with a presumption that he was protecting her. Sheryl's guilt lay in any or all of the following: not demanding that her visitor leave as soon as she learned he had the marijuana, not reporting John's purchase of the drug to the weekend house manager, and, most importantly, "seducing" Jeff into protecting her. Bob's guilt was that he told John to go ahead and smoke the marijuana because, it was assumed, at some later time he could gain John's acquiescence in his own drug use; that is, Bob had entered into a "negative contract" with John. John's guilt was by far the most straightforward in that he bought and smoked the marijuana.

These 'facts of guilt' were constructed in a group that began on Monday morning, continued through the afternoon and evening, and did not conclude until about noon on Tuesday. This Monday group thus became a "crisis" group, and it involved all the residents in the facility. The results of it were as follows: Sheryl was expelled, John was placed on a full restriction of indefinite duration (he subsequently left the program after being accused of not "properly dealing with" the restriction), Bob was placed on a thirty-day restriction, and Jeff was placed on a thirty-day restriction and formally demoted to IA status. Jeff's punishment was more severe than Bob's in that, while both were in the IP category, Bob would return to that status after serving his thirty-day restriction, whereas Jeff would have to serve his thirty days and then earn a promotion back to his IP status, which could take up to an additional thirty days. Jeff left the program several weeks later after being accused of additional rule infractions. The other "positive" residents who had participated in the Sunday group were accused of having "negative contracts," but no concrete action was taken against them; only their reputations for "positiveness" were diminished for varying lengths of time.

Incidents such as this one occur on the average of once a month. Particulars vary, but the processes, assumptions, and values are the same, and it is in such "crises" that they become most explicit. Therefore, further examination of this "crisis" can serve to illustrate the moral economy of DTF.

Sheryl's and Jeff's punishments were the most severe of all participants' because their involvement included the element of sex, and Sheryl's was more severe than Jeff's for the same reason: she "seduced" him. This interpretation was belabored throughout the one-and-a-half-day-long crisis group. Evidence to support this interpretation included information about her past based on incidents that had occurred years before she had entered DTF, in addition to observations of her conduct in the facility.

When Sheryl first entered DTF, it was demanded of her that she relate a part of her history that was dramatic, yet acknowledged to be unrelated to her drug use or her legal, probationary status. In brief, the story that she related was that some years before, her father had shot and killed her fiancé in front of her. Her father had been sent to prison, and she was emotionally traumatized. In the group discussion other residents, but especially counselors, reminded her of this story in conjunction with her relationship with Jeff. Although never explicitly stated, the story's contiguity with her supposed "seduction" of Jeff suggested that she was emotionally and morally responsible for leading her father to his violent act. This joining of biographical information to current "problems" was supported by detailed examination of her everyday interactions and conduct in the facility.

Two counselors in particular dwelled on her generally "seductive" behavior. For example, they pointed out that she often sat with her legs spread apart, and that although this was not exhibitionistic, since she was wearing trousers, not a skirt or dress, it was still "seductive." They also noted that she often rested her arms on the back of the couch or chair in which she sat, thereby presumably displaying her (clothed) breasts. There were also somewhat less specific notations of what could be called her "brazen" glances at male residents. Some of the male residents confirmed these observations; they said that they "felt" as if she had been trying to seduce them. Incidents in which she sat next to a male resident on a couch, although another seat had been vacant, were also adduced to seductive motives. In sum, a panoply of behavioral minutiae was brought forth as evidence for her character flaw of seductiveness.

Although it was one of the women who, based on subtle behavioral clues that she had picked up from him, initially brought up Jeff's attraction to Sheryl, the female residents remained noticeably silent during the attack on Sheryl for her imputed seductiveness. To enter into the discussion of seductiveness would have been risky for any woman resident because she could too easily be accused similarly, based on the same kinds of behavioral evidence used against Sheryl.

Male residents who joined in the attack on Sheryl were, so to speak, jumping on the bandwagon once the group's victim had been identified. It is not that such jumping on the bandwagon was so much a positive gain in the moral economy, but failure to jump on the bandwagon always led to suspicions: was there some sort of "negative contract" in place? Some male residents mildly defended Sheryl by saying that they did not notice her being seductive. In this case, such a position was relatively safe, because their implicit support of Sheryl could be explained as the result of Sheryl's seductiveness.

The decision to expel Sheryl was reached in consultation with her probation officer. The crucial argument used by the staff of DTF was that Sheryl was insufficiently "stable" to participate in treatment, and that it was unlikely that she would become more "stable" in the foreseeable future. Couched in these terms, her probation officer could only agree that Sheryl was "unstable," since a perceived unstable lifestyle was why she had been referred to DTF in the first place.

The severity of Jeff's punishment is only explicable given the element of sex that was brought into the picture. His decision to call together a group of residents could not in itself be such a "negative" decision, since the group process is held up as the principal means to "problem" resolution. Merely on the basis of what he *did*, his "crime" was one of poor judgment in that he did not also inform the house manager. But when his *motivation* for taking this course of action was explained as based on his attraction to Sheryl, then what he did was construed as an attempt to protect her, which is a form of "negative contract." The implication is that he would protect her in this instance in the hope of getting sexual favors from her in the future.

John's punishment was relatively standard for the offense. That he was not expelled along with Sheryl was due to some mitigation of his drug purchase—the drug was in the facility—and the fact that Bob had contributed to John's final decision to smoke the marijuana rather than throw it away or turn it over to the house manager.

Bob's punishment illustrates the great value placed on "snitching." In relating his conversation with John, he reported advising John to throw the marijuana in the toilet. Such advice was the basis for interpreting what he did as a "negative contract," and not the fact that after hours of frustrating talk, Bob told John to smoke it. Bob should have immediately reported John's possession of the drug to the house manager. Not to do so raised the possibility of receiving future favors from John, and/or entering into a future drug conspiracy with him. Hence, Bob's punishment flowed directly from not informing on John. None of the residents' moral accounts was increased as a result of this incident. Even the woman who first mentioned Jeff's attraction to Sheryl did not gain from doing so, because her failure to bring it up sooner was interpreted as contributing to the crisis. Insights about oneself or others are at best neutral, and often can be interpreted as concealing other, more nefarious motivations. The only way insights can increase residents' moral accounts is if they are submitted to public display, preferably in groups, *before* any action results from perceived motivations. And even this is insufficient, because there must be a complete account, as Jeff's experience bears witness. Furthermore, one must then submit this complete account, as it is interpreted and constructed by the group, to an authority. In this case all parties should have gone to the house manager. Since these normative expectations are impossible to put into practice—how can one define relevant motivations in the absence of the conduct on which they are premised?—residents must adopt a strategy that gives the appearance of conformity.

Residents have to discover how to express a moral commitment to the values of the program, to do so publicly, especially in groups when the most attentive staff are present, and to make sure that none of their activities outside of groups—which might contradict their protestations of commitment—are likely to be given much of a hearing. The defensive part of the strategy requires residents to be especially circumspect if they are going to break any rules of the program, even minor ones. The high, positive value placed on informing means that one cannot rely on silence from fellow residents. Nor can one rely on any form of blackmail, either implicit or explicit, since this is a "negative contract." The defensive strategy, if followed religiously, forces residents apart from one another, and those who are truly successful with it tend to be loners.

The aggressive part of the strategy can be achieved by attacking, accusing, and questioning the motives of other residents. Tone and timing are essential. Verbal assaults on other residents in the absence of staff are more likely to earn fellow residents' enmity and open one to their revenge without the gain in moral stature that is the objective of such maneuvers. It is important to carry out these attacks when one appears to derive no direct benefit from them. Throwing accusations to divert attacks on oneself is almost sure to be recognized for what it is; therefore, attacks should appear to be gratuitous. If one wishes to introduce a trump (drugs or sex) in a group, a principle of defense is to make sure that one is not holding a trump oneself. Since direct knowledge of a trump situation could constitute holding a trump, the most effective attack is one based on suspicions. This method consists of educing evidence garnered from recent past actions tied together by one's own knowledge of "dope fiend moves."

An example will give a clearer idea of how this aggressive strategy can operate. Robert is a resident who is especially adept, in part because for nine months he had been in a different therapeutic community two years before his admission to DTF. In one Monday morning group, Robert launched an attack on James, saying that the latter must have "gotten high" (used drugs and/or alcohol) while on his eight-hour weekend pass the preceding Saturday. James was already vulnerable because he had returned fifteen minutes late, and other residents were attempting to attack him because of his tardiness; however, these attacks met with little success. Much of their failure arose from the fact that the attackers had a clear self-interest: they had all voted in favor of his pass, and his late return could mean that their own pass requests for the coming weekend would be curtailed or denied. Robert, on the other hand, was not eligible for a pass for the next week and had not taken a pass the preceding week. Moreover, he had never been suspected of drug use or sex and was under no suspicion at the time of the Monday group in question. The evidence that Robert adduced to substantiate his accusation was that James had appeared "high" when he returned to the facility. Robert further claimed that he had "confronted" (i.e., accused) James at the time, but James could offer no satisfactory account of his appearance. Robert also reported his suspicions about James to the house manager.

James repeatedly denied Robert's accusations and offered an alternative explanation for his tardiness. He said that he had a heated argument with his father, and he referred to previous groups in which he had described deep-seated antagonisms between him and his father. He also gave a detailed account of all his activities while on the pass, admitting that he had been present when alcohol and drugs were consumed and that he had been offered some, but insisting that he had declined. In fact, he said, part of the argument with his father had taken place when he refused his father's insistent offer of marijuana.

After James and Robert depleted attacks and counterattacks, Robert said that he had known James had used drugs because he knew how James thought because he himself had been just like James in his earlier years and recognized James for a "dope fiend" who made "dope fiend moves." This argument put James in an indefensible position; all he could do was continue to deny the allegation. It also fore-stalled much further discussion. Everyone in the group recognized that an impasse had been reached.

This outcome is probably the best for which Robert could have hoped. He had established superior "positiveness" by demonstrating his acuity of observation, perspicacity of reasoning, and attentiveness to other residents' "problems"; he had also improved his moral status. The last had been achieved by asserting his knowledge of "dope fiend moves," implying that he could make such "moves" himself, but had made a moral choice not to.

Residents who adopt strategies similar to Robert's do not necessarily reap greater rewards by a successful attack based on imputations of drugs or sex. An attack based on any moral failing can provide the same amount of status increment. The advantages of drugs and/or sex are their trumping character, the controlling effect on interactional processes within group performances. In fact, residents are on safer ground if they rely on other topics for their accusations. Issues such as poor job performance on work crews, display of "negative attitudes," procedural irregularities, and similar issues are less likely to backfire since these issues carry less chance of the accuser having guilty knowledge.

In addition to the moral gains of successful attacks, there are more immediate, affective rewards. Generally speaking, groups in which residents are attacking each other vigorously engender a feeling of excitement among all participants, even among those who are not engaged directly in the competition. But the greatest excitement is experienced by those who are directly committed to the 'game' with its risks and rewards.

When residents attack others with whom they are on friendly terms, their emotional reactions are, predictably enough, ambivalent, while their motives are more single-minded. Attacks against friends are motivated by gains in status and, more frequently, defense against serious loss of status.

For example, one resident, Sue, was in a group largely devoted to her since she had left and then returned to the facility after spending several weeks in jail.[6] She accused a friend, Tony, of passing a note to her upon her return when no residents were permitted to communicate with her since she was on a "communications ban," a not infrequent punishment.[7] Tony's response to her attack in the group was to tell her that she "had to do what she had to do." By saying this, he was acknowledging that she was attacking him to insure her survival in the program as an alternative to going to prison. For her part, Sue deliberately chose an issue (the note passing) that she knew had been observed by other residents and therefore was likely to be used against her if she did not broach it first. Her choice also included the consideration that the rule infraction by Tony was relatively minor and that he was in the highest status group and was scheduled to graduate from the program in the fairly near future. Moreover, she could infer that Tony would interpret her attack as he did. In sum, Sue chose an incident that would not bring undue harm to her friend. Despite these precautions and mitigations, she felt guilty about the attack, and excused herself by reference to the extreme threat against her and her precarious position in the program.

Tony and Sue had developed a personal relationship grounded in extra-institutional factors. They are about the same age, have similar social characteristics, in many respects share similar background experiences, and in fact were involved in the same social network and were slightly acquainted with one another before they entered DTF. When Tony made his comment to Sue, he was calling on these outside sources of affiliation. It was as if they were actors in a play who knew each other personally and during the play made direct reference to the script.

The reaction of one of the counselors, Frank, helps illuminate this play-like construction. Frank intervened in the group directly after Tony's comment. He stated that it was Tony, not Sue, who needed the pardon of the other inasmuch as it was Tony who threatened Sue, not only by the note passing but by prior (unspecified) "negative contracts" that had contributed to Sue's departure from the program. The counselor was quite vehement when he attacked Tony, in fact he was almost screaming, as if Tony had violated some fundamental support of social life.

By his comment, Tony had pulled apart the curtains to reveal or at least question some of the illusions that sustain group performances in DTF—not wholly unlike the performance of "morning meeting" in the zoo coffee shop. Frank was calling Tony to task for his breach of the illusion, as another actor might intervene in order to return to the script instead of making reference to it. Tony's curtain-parting gesture challenged the whole framework of the moral economy by bringing forth ties that lay beyond the program.

Getting Out of Treatment

While there are a limited number of ways to get into treatment at DTF, getting out of treatment is more varied. Residents can be expelled, or they can be extracted from the program to serve some time in jail as part of the program's regime of punishment. The most common method of departure for residents is just to leave. While there are relatively few *formal* expulsions, many residents leave voluntarily with expulsion hot on their heels, so that distinctions between the two are not especially clear. No record is kept to differentiate them.

The following figures show the number of departures from DTF, either voluntary or involuntary (the numbers are those reported to the funding agency, and they are based on the daily census of the facility). Of those residents in the IA category, or the "assessment" phase of the program (more or less, the first thirty days after admission), 74 percent leave. The IP phase usually lasts for three to six months, and the GP phase for an additional one to three months. Among

IP residents, 55 percent leave, and among GP residents, 34 percent leave. The shortest time spent in the program by someone who "graduated" was seven months; the longest was fifteen months.

To put this in perspective, imagine a cohort of new admissions who fill the capacity of the facility—that is, twenty-seven admissions. Of these twenty-seven admissions, twenty leave before being promoted to the IP category. Of the seven who are promoted, slightly more than four leave sometime during their participation in this phase. That means that slightly fewer than three make it to the final phase of the program, and of those who do, only two graduate. The rate of program completion is less than 10 percent, or two out of twenty-seven. This is commensurate with national attrition rates for therapeutic communities (Simpson, 1984).

Leaving the facility either voluntarily or through expulsion can be risky for residents. Which is more risky depends on a number of variables. Since almost all residents are in DTF as a condition of probation or parole, departure prior to completion or graduation can be treated as a violation. Some residents enter the facility as a formal 'alternative to revocation,' so that upon unapproved departure their status can revert back to revocation, although they must still have an opportunity to appear for an administrative hearing prior to imprisonment. Those who do not have this formal status are still threatened with revocation proceedings. This is the basis for their initial referral by their probation officers.

Voluntary departure runs the risk that the probation officer will go ahead with revocation proceedings. On the other hand, if one has already spent a substantial amount of time in the program, the issue often becomes a matter of whether the time spent is sufficient to satisfy the probation officer. If one is expelled from the program, the resident has a defense against revocation in that it was DTF, not the resident, who terminated treatment. The problem with waiting for formal expulsion is that the resident might be jailed while awaiting disposition of revocation. This risk occurs when the program staff inform a probation officer of their intention to expel a resident and the officer comes with police to take the resident into custody without warning. Leaving the program with or without threat of expulsion does not necessarily lead to revocation, and it certainly does not entail automatic fugitive status.

Those who leave voluntarily and are not facing imminent expulsion do so to escape the onerous social control of the program. Some of those who stay fear revocation, but others stay mainly because they have no place else to go. Those who are tired of hustling on the street to survive (many are tired of it by the time they enter DTF) are willing to put up with some degree of control for some length of time as a respite from the struggle for material survival. How much control and how much time is, of course, an individual matter.

Aside from being incarcerated as a punishment, there are other more congenial ways to gain a respite from the facility. One way is the weekend pass. Residents may request passes once they have achieved IP status. Passes for IP residents can be for up to twelve hours. This time must be spent at an approved site, usually with close relatives, although some residents ask for a pass to some recreational event. In order to obtain a weekend pass, a resident must gain the approval of the majority of other IP residents. If approved by fellow residents, the pass request must then be approved by the program director, who can modify or deny the request. GP residents are eligible for twenty-four-hour passes, and these too must be approved by fellow members of the GP category as well as the director. One of the difficulties faced by residents when voting on a pass request is that, if the requestor violates some pass rule, those residents who voted in favor of the pass can have their own requests shortened or denied, depending on the severity of the violation.

A common way to gain a respite from the program is to have a legitimate appointment outside the facility. Residents have court appearances, and they must keep appointments with their probation officers. Other required appointments include medical examinations arranged by the staff. Medical and dental appointments not required by the program are somewhat more discretionary, and residents in IA are discouraged from these unless there is a specific and rather immediate medical need. Outside appointments that are not required by law or are not arranged by the staff are treated as discretionary to some degree, depending on the specific circumstances.

There are two other ways to go out of treatment, at least temporarily. One is through the "privileges" of twenty-minute walks and/or being "off the floor." The "off the floor" privilege entitles residents to go to their bedrooms for two hours no more than once per day, if they have no other obligations—for example, participating in a work crew or attending educational classes. These "privileges" are accorded to all GP residents on account of their status; IP residents must earn them through the point system in the "privilege meeting," and IA residents are not eligible.

Residents can also be out of treatment metaphorically. Being out of treatment in the metaphorical sense means to be "unstable" or not making "progress" in treatment. This is tantamount to punishment that is ostensibly designed to get residents back into treatment.

The most unusual way to leave DTF is to graduate or complete the program. In addition to having gained sufficient moral stature to be considered rehabilitated, residents must meet some objective criteria. They must have an acceptable residence, either their own or with close relatives. They must have a job or be in school full time, and they must have adequate income to be self-supporting.

Residents 'walk the walk and talk the talk' by playing the treatment game. Playing this game is manifest in various performances, both those that are framed relatively formally, such as groups, and those everyday interactions that make up the stuff of life. How each resident plays this game is a matter of individual style conditioned by idiosyncratic life histories, motivations, and goals; but play it they must if they are to survive in the program.

On the surface, performances of the residents may appear simply as attempts to conform to an imposed regimentation, but playing the game is not a simple matter of conformity. Resident performances embody resistance to regimentation as much as conformity to it. The performances are the way residents escape control as they try to gain advantages in the moral economy.

The performances of the residents are conditioned in part by the material reality of the facility—its political economy. This conditioning framework is explicated in Chapter 4. However, much of this material reality is subject to massive repression and disguise so that it remains obscure for residents and counselors alike. In contrast, the explicit ideology of the program is consciously articulated.

The most important social objects for residents in DTF are the staff members, especially the counselors. From the residents' perspective, it is their relationship to the counselors that determines the playing of the treatment game. Therefore, the experiences and points of view of the counselors are addressed in the next chapter.

CHAPTER 3

The Counselors

P EOPLE WHO BECOME COUNSELORS at DTF get the job the same way people get most white-collar jobs: by answering "Help Wanted" advertisements in the newspaper or hearing about a job opening through the grapevine. Criteria for employment are rather broad. Counselors should have training or experience in some human service field. There are no specific educational requirements, no licensing or certification requirements, and no particular kind of human service background is favored over others, except for drug counseling experience per se.

How to Become a Drug Counselor

Compared with other organizations that provide drug treatment, DTF has relatively undefined prerequisites for its counselors. Most other treatment providers require that their counselors be certified by a state board, be well on their way to certification, or have some equivalent training. DTF's lack of such requirements is a holdover from the time when counselors were really just senior residents in the facility. Hiring criteria are informal and less than explicit. Probably the most important of these is that counselors should not be current drug abusers. This requirement does not preclude employment of previous drug abusers. In fact, it is believed to be desirable to have at least one ex-addict counselor on the staff. The criterion for being considered an ex-addict is at least two years' abstinence. This is the same criterion used for certification by the state board. While applicants for counselor positions who identify themselves as ex-addicts are questioned rather intensively about present and previous drug use, those who do not so identify themselves are simply asked whether they consume illicit drugs or have any kind of "drug problem."

Other important, informal criteria relate to staff demographics. A "balance" is sought for gender and race among the four counselors.

One other informal criterion is that counselors should not appear to be overly committed to one particular theory or method of counseling. Ideal counselors are those who identify their technique as "eclectic," but a preference for or training in a method is all right as long as the prospective counselor seems to be "flexible," and not "rigid" or "rabidly dedicated" to one particular approach.

This prejudice against specific therapeutic methodology derives from the tradition of therapeutic communities that originally were outside of institutionalized clinical professions. It reflects a historical anti-professional attitude that is subtle but pervasive. Although this prejudice is especially evident at DTF, it is not too different from a similar pragmatism and anti-theoretical attitude in the drug counseling field in general. For instance, the drug counselors' certification handbook says, "The role and function of these counselors has evolved from many years of experience in counseling drug abusers and achieving desired results." The principal criterion is "achieving desired results" with relatively little concern about methodological particulars.

Pragmatism, anti-professionalism, and relatively indeterminate hiring criteria combine with relatively low salaries to make the position of counselor at DTF an entry-level job for people who plan to work in human service careers. Overall, positions in drug treatment are more or less equivalent to those in other human service fields, but compared to other drug treatment organizations, DTF offers one of the lowest salaries. Starting pay for a counselor was about $13,000 a year in 1986, and the highest pay for a counselor was less than $20,000. The director receives less than $25,000. The low pay contributes to a high turnover among counselors. Since the facility was purchased by the present administration in 1979, only one counselor had remained at DTF for much more than two years.

High turnover and the fact that DTF tends to be an entry-level organization for counselors mean that it provides the initial socialization in the occupation for most of the counseling staff. Therefore, most DTF counselors have no basis for comparison with other clinical situations. It would not be far from wrong to say that residents often have more familiarity with drug treatment than do counselors.

Once hired, counselors are required to work toward certification. Although certification brings only a slight raise in pay, it enables DTF counselors to get higher-paying jobs elsewhere in the drug counseling field. Because the career ladder for counselors within DTF is so limited, increased experience, training, and certification are lost to the facility as its counselors move to other jobs.

During my fieldwork at DTF, the director was the only one left from the staff of the facility before its purchase by the present administration. He had been in other therapeutic communities before coming to this facility. He was a certified counselor and had a two-year degree from a technical-vocational community college.

Two counselors had left just before I began work at DTF. One was an ex-addict counselor who, soon after he received his certification, moved to another program administered by the parent agency. The other had received her master's degree in clinical social work, and this had been her first job in a treatment setting. She too moved on to another program within the agency as soon as she received certification as both a drug counselor and a clinical social worker.

The one exception to the two-year rule was a counselor who had worked at DTF for four years, although he finally left several months after my arrival. He had an undergraduate degree in philosophy, had been employed by the agency in several other programs that it administered, and had obtained his drug counselor certification while working at DTF.

Three counselors were hired during my tenure at the facility. One was an ex-addict who had not completed high school but had obtained a high-school equivalency certificate. She obtained her drug counseling certification, and shortly thereafter found employment in a different drug treatment organization. The second counselor had an undergraduate degree in psychology and had performed volunteer work facilitating discussion groups of imprisoned sex offenders. The third had done some graduate work in education. DTF was her first experience in a treatment situation. I left the facility while these latter two were still employed there.

What Counselors Do

Tasks of counselors at DTF fall into three broad domains, which I designate as follows: supervision, casework, and liaison. Supervision can be so called because it consists mainly of supervising social interaction within the facility—running group therapy, enforcing rules, and generally affirming the moral order. Casework refers to the work of counselors with their assigned caseload—residents for whom counselors are "primary therapists." Casework consists of one-on-one "counseling sessions," treatment planning, and, generally speaking, "individualized treatment."

These first two domains pertain to relations between residents and counselors. The third domain, liaison, refers to relations among counselors and interactions with people outside the facility in which the counselor acts as an agent of DTF. Liaison is most important because counselors learn their jobs first and foremost from other counselors and from interactions with outsiders. Almost immediately, counselors are confronted with situations in which they must exercise their authority over the lives of residents, because residents ask counselors for various kinds of permission—for example, to make a telephone call, to leave the facility on some errand, or to go "off the floor." Therefore, one of the first things counselors must learn is the extent of their authority.

Counselors have the authority to override any rule except the four "cardinal" rules (no drugs, sex, violence, or disclosure of "treatment information"). However, counselors should be able to justify any decision to override a rule by referring to some criterion of treatment. This means that they have to know what constitutes treatment according to the other counselors. They have to know how other counselors view residents; they have to learn the narratives and discourses other counselors have constructed about particular residents. While much of this kind of information is imparted and obtained in casual interactions among counselors, it is communicated most intensively in staff meetings.

Staff meetings are held twice a week and typically last for two to three hours. Once or twice a month the consulting psychologist attends the meetings, but usually only the counselors and the director attend. These occasions are formal versions of the counselor-to-counselor interaction that one finds throughout the day.

Two conditions of staff meetings are especially relevant: the structuring of the occasion and the form of discourse about residents. In the staff meeting, counselors are set apart, and residents are excluded. Whether in a formal staff meeting or in less formal gatherings of counselors, counselor space is bounded. In the case of the staff meetings, counselors meet in the general purpose room of the second floor with the doors closed. Separation is assured not only by the closed doors but also by the fact that the second floor is empty of residents during the daytime because it is "off the floor." Similar spatial boundaries are achieved in informal gatherings by meeting in a staff office or in out-of-the-way places such as stairwells. The reason for this privacy is supposed to be confidentiality, although this is hard to reconcile with the persistent emphasis on publicizing residents' personal lives in groups. Another, more plausible reason is that it allows counselors a sense of freedom of expression.

The other condition commonly found in staff meetings is a focus and stress on psychological and individualistic constructions of residents and their conduct. It is significant that the only regular outsider in these meetings is the consulting psychologist, who is called upon to provide psychological assessments of selected residents. Discussions of group dynamics are conspicuously absent. Reports and interpretations of interactions are always phrased so as to treat interactants as independent subjects. The interactions are discussed in terms of what they reveal about the parties, with no reference to the broader context. It is as if residents interacted with one another and with staff members in a completely neutral situation that experimental social psychologists would envy.

In these meetings counselors adopt a very objective form of conversation about residents. It is replete with passive-voice constructions and third-person reference; one would almost think these were oral ethnographies. Some of this has to do with the fact that the form of case presentations is a frequent rhetorical device. Case presentations are formally used when a resident is promoted from the Assessment to the Intermediate category. Here, the "primary therapist" reports on the "assessment" and proposes a treatment plan. Other counselors are invited to comment on both the assessment and the treatment plan, although it is rare that the "primary therapist's" judgment is substantively questioned. This rhetorical form virtually demands an individualistic and psychological focus, but the focus prevails throughout the meeting whenever residents are the topic of discussion.

These conditions of counselor interaction convey an important lesson: '*We* counselors view *those* residents as individuals in need of individualized treatment.' The counselors are a collectivity, but the residents are individuals. This viewpoint is reinforced by the most common kinds of contact that counselors have with outside agents.

The most frequent contact is with probation officers, who tend to have interests in specific residents. More often than not, residents have been admitted to DTF in response to a referral by a probation officer. These agents of the state correctional system have the primary responsibility to maintain surveillance on persons assigned to them. Therefore, when they refer people to DTF, they expect the facility to provide that surveillance. Secondarily, probation officers are expected to control the behavior of their charges, and so they pass the same expectation on to DTF. Given the fact that DTF is a twenty-four-hour residential facility, it can do a much more thorough job of both surveillance and control, and this is what probation officers demand.

Whether a resident is 'cured' of drug addiction, or any other malady, is of tertiary concern to probation officers. Whatever their personal feelings may be in regard to therapy, their jobs and their supervisors require that they keep their caseload under control. It looks bad for a probation officer to have very many people in a 'whereabouts unknown' status, or to have probationers caught for crimes. One of the main reasons that probation officers refer people to DTF is that persons who are so referred are high-risk probationers. It is important to remember that many admissions come out of jail, so either the individual has been arrested for a crime or the probation officer has put the person in custody with the possibility of revocation of probation or parole. Revocation is a time-consuming and demanding task, especially if the case for revocation is questionable. Referral to DTF can be a solution to the problems of a probation officer in these circumstances.[1] Therefore, referral to DTF shifts the responsibility of supervision from the probation officer to this facility with the hope that sev-

eral months of residency here will get the probationer to
'settle down.'

The important point of probation officer involvement in
DTF is that the officers' interests are attached to individual
cases. They have little concern with therapeutic processes,
but rather with the effect DTF has on their particular probationers. Most immediately officers are interested in ensuring
that the probationer will remain in the facility. It is this interest that contributed to reducing the harshness of the intake process for new admissions: persons who anticipate
that the regime in DTF will be too 'tough' are likely to leave
the facility, thus defeating the main purpose of the referral.
Probation officers often can be persuaded to cooperate with
DTF processes by lending credence to the power of DTF
staff through threats or by actually taking a resident into
custody as part of a punishment.[2]

Other outside agents (e.g., bail monitors, public de-
fenders, prosecutors) have interests similar to those of probation officers, since almost all of them are in some way
part of the criminal justice system. That is, their interests are
case-specific and pertain to surveillance and control. These
outside agents are important for the maintenance of DTF,
because the facility depends on them for referrals. These
'facts of life' are an important part of the socialization process for counselors.

State licensure of DTF requires that each resident's file
have a written treatment plan. These treatment plans are
supposed to aim at habilation or rehabilitation based on
the assessed deficiencies of individual residents. In the case
of DTF, because it is a facility that treats drug abuse, the
assessment and treatment plan should be related to the "disability" of drug abuse and its related consequences. Additional deficiencies may of course be noted, but these are not
the kinds of things that the inspector looks for. The inspector also reviews case notes and progress reports, which are
supposed to be part of each resident's file. These too should
be related to the assessment and treatment plan.

State inspectors do not actually observe activities in the facility. Their review of treatment procedures is strictly a 'paper' review. Therefore, adherence to written assessments and treatment plans leaves a great deal of latitude between what is written and what actually occurs. That some counselors are scrupulous about adhering to these documents while others are not makes little practical difference. For instance, a common 'deficiency' for most residents is employment. Failure to obtain regular employment would be the deficiency, vocational skills would be the goal of treatment, and referral to a vocational training program would be the relevant treatment intervention. How a counselor pursues the matter of employment involves a rather broad continuum. "Referral to a vocational training program" can take the form of telling the resident to apply to the state department of vocational rehabilitation, at one end of the continuum, or it may involve active teaching and job finding on behalf of the resident at the other extreme.

More or less objective treatment goals such as vocational preparation are considered emergent by most counselors. They are emergent in the sense that most counselors believe that vocational deficits (and other, similar objective problems) experienced by residents are the outcome of the "dope fiend" lifestyle and "addict personality" attributed to residents. Bringing about change *within* individual residents is the first and most important task of treatment from the counselors' point of view. Once such internal change is achieved, or at least underway, remedies for problems such as employment are assumed to be relatively simple.

This viewpoint is consistently reinforced among counselors by attending to residents' beliefs, motivations, attitudes, and values as these are based on observation of residents' conduct in the facility. The premise here is similar to that on which psychological tests are based. Careful evaluation of a particular 'slice of life'—for example, performance on a test or, in the case of DTF, conduct in therapy groups—reveals some guiding, internal pattern or principle within individuals. The diagnostic or assessment function of counselors is to identify the idiosyncratic variation of the basic character flaws intrinsic to addict personalities. Individual treatment is then geared to these idiosyncratic variations in what is an ostensibly similar overall personality pattern. Identifying idiosyncracies is the principal focus of assessment and treatment. It is what counselors talk about among themselves, and it is what shapes their interactions with residents.

Understanding these presumed personality problems in residents permits any number of psychological theories. As far as case conferences (both formal and informal) are concerned, a counselor may adopt any theory or combination of theories. It matters little whether a counselor constructs assessment and treatment according to theories such as social learning, cognitive-behaviorism, gestalt, or transactional analysis. The reason that theoretical differences are relatively insignificant is that conduct of both counselors and residents must conform to the treatment program of the facility. This conformity means that theories take on the character of rationalizations for doing what the program demands. Therefore, it is the supervisory function or domain that determines the limits of the casework domain.

Rules are the main technique of the treatment program in DTF. Sooner or later all actions by counselors devolve to regulation. This may consist of interpretation, modification, formulation, abrogation, explanation, enforcement, but whatever the form of the act, it ultimately comes down to rules. There are rules for virtually every conceivable aspect of life for residents. There are rules for dressing, for bathroom use, for eating, for sleeping, for talking, and so on. Most of these rules are not written, and counselors are the ultimate authority for them.

Even more than residents, counselors must learn the rules by inference. While residents are told many rules by senior residents and sometimes by staff members, there is little opportunity for such explicit learning by counselors.

Counselors must learn the rules by observing residents and other staff members. Since there are far too many rules covering all kinds of ordinary minutiae for any counselor to learn each rule separately, the learning process for counselors relies heavily on the construction of meta-rules such as those governing hygiene, dress, and deportment. One observes that most residents are in casual but neat and clean attire. A resident who does not conform is notified by another resident that she or he will be brought "to council" (the resident disciplinary body) for wearing a shirt outside of the trousers instead of tucked in. Another resident is brought "to council" for wearing a "pick" (a long, wide-toothed comb with no handle) with the further admonition that such "street" wear is not suitable here. The slightly swaggering gait of another resident is also cited as a rule violation. The meta-rule to be constructed from such observations need not be one that is easily stated explicitly; for example, the one that I formulated was that residents should look and act as if they are at a perpetual job interview.

Ironically, residents expect counselors to be completely conversant with all rules within a week or so after beginning employment and to give them definitive interpretations and applications. These expectations put pressure on counselors to exert effort and attention into formulating their meta-rules as an important part of their job responsibilities. This inferential construction of rules leads inevitably to the counselors' socialization into basic assumptions and values of the program. Almost without realizing it, counselors have to adopt a programmatic attitude in order to make their meta-rules.

Rules offer counselors a degree of release from responsibility. As mentioned, counselors are constantly asked for various kinds of 'permissions.' Special permission to make a telephone call outside the guidelines is a frequent kind of request. Rather than trying to keep track of all the telephone rules (which seem to change monthly) as well as the particulars of every resident's status and privileges, counselors can just adhere to the 'letter of the law.' Moreover, when there is a request for some kind of exception to a rule, counselors risk second-guessing by other counselors. For example, a resident may ask to go to a medical appointment outside the facility without "strength." While surface appearances might lead one to grant this request, if the resident breaks a rule while on this appointment (e.g., by making a telephone call or buying a pack of cigarettes or committing a crime), part of the responsibility redounds on the counselor. It is much safer, then, to go with the rules.

Rules also frame individual counseling. As with diagnosis and treatment plans, counselors may use a variety of psychological theories, treatment methodologies, and therapeutic techniques, but what counts for residents in the program is always defined in terms of rules. "Progress in treatment" is a matter of "problem resolution," and no matter what the "problem" may be, it is always transformed into residents' relationships to rules. Problems that seem, at first blush, to be quite distant from the rules can be so transformed.

A striking instance of how a medical need was transformed into a rule issue is the case of a resident who complained of abdominal distress. After a preliminary medical examination, he was scheduled for a complete gastro-intestinal X-ray series at the county hospital. He was reluctant to have this performed because he feared the enema that is part of the procedure. He explained that he had been anally raped while in prison, and that that was the reason for his reluctance. He was required to have the examination, and this requirement was stated in terms of rules that required residents to "resolve medical problems." In this case, the decisive issue became a question of the resident following the rules of the program.

Not only are there rules that require "problem resolution"; there are rules that describe how residents should go about this task. A significant number of residents have histories of physical and/or sexual abuse as children. The principal way such "problems" are supposed to be "resolved" is by talking about the incidents and histories in groups. There is always some risk for residents in this kind of self-disclosure, because once they have revealed the information, it can be used as an 'explanation' for their own rule violations. For instance, a resident who is perceived to be intimidating would be told that this "problem" was caused by the fact that s/he had been abused as a child. This is representative of the basic strategy of 'counseling' that is thought to be efficacious. The more immediate "problems" that a counselor can identify in a resident (almost always rule violations) and the more these immediate "problems" can be related to persistent or historical "problems" of the resident, the more the resident can "resolve" the problems by making them public. This is the nature of the "progress in treatment" under the guidance of counselors.

Another part of counselors' interaction with individual residents pertains to rule enforcement and punishment. The "primary therapist" of a resident is usually the one who determines the specifics of any kind of "restriction." "Restrictions" are written documents that follow a form. The form is filled out by the "primary therapist" in consultation with the resident, and the resident signs it. A facsimile of this form follows.

INDIVIDUAL RESIDENT RESTRICTION FORM

The object of this written restriction explanation is to clearly identify the problems resulting in the restriction, and to also identify the individual conditions during the restriction period. The resident should use this to address or solve the initial problems, and to answer questions about movement, privileges and limitations during the restriction period.

This restriction period shall last for _____ day(s)/week(s) beginning on _____ and ending on _____. This restriction will/will not be reviewed, and may continue longer based on that review.

The reasons for the restriction are:

The problems needing resolution are:

Measurement of the problem solving efforts will be:

Conditions of the restriction are:
Counseling (define)
Job assignment change (define)
Other

Limits of the restriction are:
phone calls
passes/visits
outside appointments
strength
recreational activities (ind. vs. group)
privileges (define)
other

I understand the above and agree to participate:

          Resident Signature _____

          Staff Witness _____

The rather legalistic character of the restriction format—the use of 'shall' and the resident signature with a witness—is not happenstance. Restrictions are intended to be regulatory and *therapeutic because they are regulatory*. Restrictions are believed to be an important instrument of counseling, much more so than what elsewhere might be called 'therapeutic technique.' Individual counselors are accorded the privilege of using a wide variety of techniques and methods, but among the counseling staff such variation is considered to be a matter of individual style. The way counselors handle "restrictions" is thought to be far more representative of their counseling skill.

The most pervasive supervisional function of counselors is achieved by their presence in the facility. Just being there and observing residents are important parts of the job. This effect of presence operates in a way similar to the presence of police outside the facility. Police presence is thought by some to deter crime; analogously, counselor presence is thought to deter rule violations and thus to contribute to "progress in treatment" for all residents. It is noteworthy that counselors constantly seem to be denying the notion that they are cops or that they want to act like cops; this denial is followed by the assertion that the behavior of the residents is what forces them to act like cops.

CONTRADICTIONS AND CONFLICTS

There are two areas in which counselors face contradictions and conflicts: one is the conflicting demands of their functions inside the facility, and the other is their position in the facility with respect to the world outside of it. This second area of conflict is one that counselors in DTF share with other people who work in the field of drug abuse treatment. The conflict arises from a belief in the contaminating effect of drug abuse. People who work in the field become suspect of the corruption attributed to those whom they treat.

The notion is that drugs offer forbidden pleasure—special ecstatic gratification—and that they appeal to the animal pleasure-seeking in everyone. The price one pays for this gratification is not only ill health and loss of property but most importantly, moral corruption. Drugs take away the essence of personhood, the individual will. It is for this reason that drug addicts are presumed to have dependent personalities. Some treatment providers are ex-addicts, and there is always the risk that an ex-addict is not quite so 'ex.' Drug abusers also are believed to be especially adept at manipulating other people. Through deceit, dissimulation, conniving, and "conning," addicts are thought to be able to get other people to do what they want them to do. To work

with addicts exposes a person to being manipulated into
complicity with their corruption.

This issue of manipulation is important in the field of
drug treatment in general, and at DTF in particular. From
other counselors, from functionaries from outside agencies
(e.g., probation officers), and even from the residents themselves, counselors quickly learn the danger of being manipulated by residents. On my first day as a counselor, one of the
residents warned me that they were a "pretty slick group."
Any time a resident asks for any kind of special consideration, or when a resident breaks a rule, s/he is likely to be
accused of being manipulative.

Wariness about manipulation is connected with the belief that counselors must control residents. Pressure on
counselors to control residents comes from external sources
such as probation officers and from the counselors' own desire not to be manipulated. Of course, the more counselors
try to control residents, the more residents are pushed toward resisting that control in ways that tend to be interpreted as manipulative.

Manipulation is taken to be a sign of a dependent personality, which is the main character flaw attributed to addicts. The primary target of counselors' therapeutic efforts is
supposed to be the amelioration of dependency. Therefore,
on therapeutic grounds, counselors should not let themselves be manipulated. There is yet another twist here that
makes the counselors' position even more conflictual. The
way counselors must resist manipulation is by dispensing
the belief that the community of residents is the decisive
agent in the residents' treatment and eventual rehabilitation.
Individualized treatment takes a back seat to treatment in
and by 'the community.' And the principal means used by
counselors to effect 'community' treatment is enforcing the
rules of the program.

Counselors are not aware of their role as repressive
agents who must 'keep the lid on' oppositional potential
among residents. Neither do they see their dependence on

the performances of residents when counselors interpret rules and program ideology. This ideological dependence is in no mean way related to the economic dependency of the counselors on the residents. Almost completely repressed is the fact that the counselors' salaries are paid through the presence of residents in the facility. How this political economy works is the subject of the next chapter.

CHAPTER 4

The Political Economy

T HERE ARE THREE WAYS to analyze the political economy of DTF: from the outside, from the inside, and historically. From the outside, DTF is a public health service. This service is financed from the federal, state, and county levels of government by a variety of budgetary allotments through social service programs. From the inside it looks like a domestic site—a household in which residents are dependents, and administrators are the heads. From a historical point of view, the economic system of the facility appears as a strategy to multiply the drug treatment industry.

THE OUTSIDE VIEW

Public policy identifies drug addiction as a disability. DTF is in a state that statutorily mandates a system for providing services to those persons who are disabled by alcohol or other drug abuse as well as by mental illness or developmental disabilities. These categories are defined by administrative regulation. The system provides for an agency to operate at the local level of government. In urban areas, the county is the local unit. Federal, state, and local funds derived from a variety of public health and social service programs are funneled into this county agency, which then makes contracts with direct service providers to meet the needs of persons categorically identified as disabled. DTF is one such provider, although in this case the contract is between the county funding agency and the larger social service agency of which DTF is a part.

Food stamps and money that comes from the county disability funding agency cover almost all the budget for DTF. An indeterminate proportion of the administrative overhead of the parent agency of DTF comes from private charity, but this is not a direct cost and in any case is a very small part of the DTF budget. The total annual budget is about $242,000 plus an estimated $23,000 in food stamps.[1] The purchase-of-service contract with the county agency is based on "units of service." The "unit of service" in the case of DTF is a resident-day, a day of residency of one person. The contract calls for twenty-three such units per day and twenty-seven units per day per month. From year to year, the contract is 10 to 15 percent under the actual census of the facility. Excluding food stamps, the unit cost of service is $28.82 per day per resident.

Residential treatment is more effective and more efficient than the two other treatment modalities purchased by the county funding agency. Inpatient hospital treatment is $125 per day per patient, while outpatient counseling is $14.52 per quarter hour (the unit of service for this modality), or about $78.00 per hour for individuals, and the rate for group counseling is $7.26 per quarter hour, or $29.00 per hour.[2]

While there are a great many superficial differences among them, these three treatment modalities are in fact commensurable. Inpatient treatment usually encompasses a twenty-one-day program.[3] The twenty-one-day program is fairly standard because that is what private health insurers pay for. Although inpatient treatment provides medically supervised detoxification (i.e., observation during withdrawal), detoxification can be accomplished outside of a hospital, as it was in a few cases at DTF. For example, detoxification from heroin is treated with methadone. The dosage of methadone is gradually decreased and in most cases, complete detoxification is achieved in fourteen days. On two admittedly unusual occasions, residents of DTF detoxified from heroin by means of an outpatient methadone program. Detoxification from cocaine is often carried out without benefit of medical supervision, and, in fact, for many DTF residents, so is heroin detoxification since many of them detoxify in jail. Detoxification from alcohol and pharmaceuticals such as benzodiazepines can present medical dangers, but treatment for medical emergencies (as opposed to medical supervision) is not provided in the inpatient drug treatment facility; instead patients are temporarily transferred to general hospitals.

Aside from the medical supervision, inpatient treatment consists of group and individual counseling and a structured daily regimen. In other words inpatient treatment has the same form as that of residential programs except that residential programs have physicians and nurses and some hospital equipment.

Obviously, outpatient programs differ from residential programs in that outpatients are not sequestered. The counseling itself is much the same, based on the same principles, the same understanding of addiction and treatment for it, and it can include a degree of surveillance in the form of urinalysis. Outpatient counseling can be conceived as a less intensive form of residential treatment. Another outpatient treatment modality should be mentioned, although it is specific for heroin addiction, namely, methadone maintenance. Unlike the other three modalities, methadone maintenance does not aim at abstinence from drugs, since treatment consists of providing methadone as a replacement drug for heroin. The cost of methadone treatment is twenty-five dollars to two hundred dollars per month, depending on the particular program. This cost includes only the administration of the drug. While methadone maintenance programs discourage patients from taking other drugs, enforcement is notoriously lax.

Residential treatment appears to be the most effective treatment modality. While inpatient treatment keeps patients away from drugs for only twenty-one days, residential treatment can provide a relatively drug-free environment for many months. Outpatient counseling can do little to insure abstinence outside of urinalysis checks. Outpatients who wish to conceal their drug use often defeat this kind of surveillance, and the laboratory procedures themselves are not entirely reliable.

If the most immediate objective of drug treatment is abstinence, an assumption upon which the county funding agency operates, residential treatment yields the greatest effectiveness for the least cost. In sum, residential treatment gives the biggest bang for the buck. Moreover, among residential programs DTF is the least expensive, although the difference in treatment cost is much less than among different treatment modalities. Two other residential facilities have costs of $39.05 and $34.75 per day compared to DTF's $28.82 per day. DTF can also be compared to the cost of jail since this facility is an alternative to incarceration for most residents. Jail is far more expensive. The daily cost is $51.64, and between $39.16 and $97.02 for prison. The range reflects costs for a minimum security facility at the low end and a maximum security facility at the high end.

The penal system and the disability system have fundamentally different fiscal structures. Money for the penal system is attached to institutional sites whether these be carceral facilities or agencies such as the office of probation and parole. These sites contain persons subject to the system. In contrast, the disability system attaches money to persons in much the same way as health insurance does. The county disability funding agency does not pay for DTF as an institutional site; it reimburses DTF for services rendered to individuals.

While the different fiscal structures may appear to have the same effects, the implications are entirely different from an administrative point of view. For a penal administrator, the fiscal problem is one of over-demand on the system; for a disabilities administrator the problem is under-demand. In practical terms at DTF, the administrative objective is to have an average daily census above twenty-three, since the service contract pays for twenty-three "treatment slots." If DTF falls below that number on an annual basis, it must return money to the funding agency. On the other hand, if over a period of several years DTF consistently operates above the contracted number of "slots," the program has grounds for requesting an increase in its contract. This means that one of the most important economic exigencies for DTF is recruitment of residents: it must have a continual supply of people with money attached to them.

An interesting paradox arises as a result of the fiscal structure of the disabilities system. From the perspective of the funding agency, in total there are too few "treatment slots" in the county to meet the demand for services. The funding agency's administration has a problem similar to that of the penal administration—over-demand—because the funding agency has a limit on its total budget. At the same time, DTF flourishes, in an economic sense, in a situation of over-demand, because then it has greater control over recruitment. For DTF, a waiting list is desirable, but for the funding agency, waiting lists for service programs are undesirable.

By relying on the correctional system, DTF is in an ideal niche in the institutional ecological system. It has no competitors for criminalized drug addicts. The chronic over-demand for jail space generates a continuous supply of potential residents, and this in turn means that DTF can be selective in its admissions. It also means that residents can be admitted when DTF is ready to receive them, not when they are ready to enter.

In contrast, consider another residential facility that gets most of its referrals from inpatient hospital treatment programs. This program has to coordinate admissions with discharges from twenty-one-day inpatient programs. Since inpatient programs have little elasticity, this residential program also has little elasticity. DTF, on the other hand, can take its time with admissions from the correctional system, because people can always stay in jail a little longer.

A major concern of the funding agency is the revolving door effect. The revolving door effect swells demand for drug treatment services when people who have received treatment return to using drugs and then request treatment again. While this agency keeps no records that would give an accurate representation of the impact of the revolving door effect, administrators in the agency believe that it makes a large contribution to over-demand for services. Therefore, the funding agency strives for permanent or relatively permanent cure. The revolving door has little direct impact on DTF. Unlike inpatient programs, re-admissions to DTF have a cycle of years rather than months. The funding agency operates on an annual cycle; data from year to year are meager. As a result, DTF has a very low re-admission rate compared to other treatment programs, at least as far as funding records indicate.

One of the solutions to the revolving door effect favored by the funding agency is the continuum of care. This concept assumes that rehabilitation from drug addiction takes place over a period of time divided into stages. In each stage, recipients of services have different needs: initially they may need inpatient care for detoxification, then a residential program to prevent rapid return to addiction, then outpatient supportive counseling, vocational rehabilitation, social casework, and so on. In keeping with its policy to establish a continuum of care, the funding agency encourages its contractees to extend their services. It also encourages them to seek alternative funds to carry out this extension.

The therapeutic community concept of treatment within which DTF operates is conceived of as a complete treatment program containing all elements of rehabilitation. To extend services is incompatible with this concept because it is viewed as redundant. While there is some recognition of what is called "aftercare" by DTF, this consists of referral to an outpatient counseling program; it is not seen as an integral part of residential treatment.

One of the extensions encouraged by the funding agency is vocational rehabilitation. Since DTF includes work and/or school in the final phase of the program, it claims that this program component is already in place. Similarly, it interprets the encouragement to seek alternative sources of funds as requiring working residents to contribute a greater proportion of their earnings toward their cost of care. However, the high attrition rate means that relatively few DTF residents ever contribute earnings.

In any case, this form of vocational rehabilitation is not what the funding agency has in mind. They envision a new program component, funded perhaps by a special grant, that would involve residents in vocational preparation early in their treatment. These conflicting conceptions lead to an impasse between DTF and the funding agency, and an attitude on the part of the latter that DTF is an inflexible "old-style" program. Repeated requests by DTF to increase funding are viewed as intensification rather than extension of services; therefore they are rejected.

Viewed from the outside, then, DTF occupies a secure niche, but one that allows no growth. Its dependence on the correctional system provides a stable source of residents and therefore of continued funding. However, it is perceived as representing an old-fashioned, uninnovative technology, in no way a model for new treatment programs.

THE INSIDE VIEW

None of this is visible from the inside. The internal economy of DTF is a household economy. Matching this, the ideological construct of DTF is a "family." One might imagine this domestic economy as analogous to that of a large bourgeois family household in the early part of this century.

The program administrator is the patriarch, whose 'work' supports all the other dependents. He or she is the one who negotiates the contract with the funding agency, and with the local welfare agency for food stamps. Although absent much of the time, he or she does make appearances but is a rather distant figure for most residents and staff members. The staff (counselors and house managers), while they would fit the maternal role, are not wives to the administrator, so for imaginative purposes, they can be pictured as the hired governess in lieu of an absent wife-mother. As in the case of such a governess or housekeeper, they depend on the 'work' of the administrator for their salaries. Also, as in the case of a governess, their role vis-à-vis the children (residents) is one of management, of discipline, caretaking, and overall supervision.

In this model, the residents are the children with their assigned tasks to perform in support of the domestic unit. There is an ethic of egalitarianism among these children (residents), with differentiation primarily made on the basis of age (seniority in the program). This differentiation is grounded in moral terms, not other kinds of social markers.

The domestic labor of the residents under this model is interesting because it is entirely unwaged; in fact it is in a special category known as "therapeutic work." It is crucial to have a special category like this one in order to get around laws restricting the labor of inmates in asylums—laws that derive from the reforms enacted in the early part of this century. Both federal and state statutes prohibit the employment of inmates to further the fiscal position of the institution in which they are housed. However, designating the labor of residents as a therapeutic activity makes it possible to employ them without pay.

Upon entering DTF, all residents must acknowledge awareness and understanding of their rights as guaranteed by state statute and regulations. They acknowledge understanding by signing the form entitled "Client Rights and Complaint Procedure," after the following statement: "I understand them fully [the rights and complaint procedures], and realize that if I believe any of my rights are being violated, I am entitled to utilize the complaint procedure to pursue resolution." The list of client rights follows.

1. The right to be informed of the Clients Bill of Rights.

2. The right to confidentiality of conversations and medical records.

3. The right to receive wages for work performed which involves the operation and maintenance of the facility except for matters of personal care, i.e., making one's own bed, scheduled assignments, etc.

4. The right to petition a court according to law.

5. The right to maintain the rights of citizens, i.e., voting, marriage, obtain a driver's license, etc.

6. The right to receive prompt and adequate treatment.

7. The right to receive medication and treatment on a voluntary basis prior to court hearing or commitment.

8. The right to the least restrictive treatment conditions necessary.

9. The right to have an informal hearing prior (except in emergencies) to being transferred to a more restrictive ward, unit or facility.

10. The right to be free from unnecessary or excessive medication.

11. The right to be free from physical restraint or involuntary isolation.

12. The right not to receive psychosurgery, electroconvulsive treatment, adversive conditioning, etc.

13. The right not to participate in experimental research.

14. The right to religious worship.

15. The right to humane psychological and physical environment.

16. The right to send and receive sealed mail and to use a telephone.

17. The right to select, use and wear own clothing, etc.

18. The right to have individual storage space for private use.

19. The right to privacy in dressing, toiletting, and bathing.

20. The right to receive visitors.

One of the rights (number 3 on the form) is "The right to receive wages for work performed which involves the operation and maintenance of the facility except for matters of personal care, i.e., making one's own bed, scheduled assignments, etc." All residents receive a copy of this form.

Of course, many of the "client rights" are irrelevant in the daily operation of DTF; it is clear to everyone that there is no real threat that a resident will be subject to psychosurgery, for example (number 12 on the form). A few residents upon rare occasion have lodged formal complaints based on perceived violations of some of the "client rights." But no one ever complained about not receiving wages for work that supports the maintenance of the facility, despite the fact that everyone is so employed.

Even to the casual observer, tasks performed by residents far exceed "matters of personal care," yet the contribution to the "operation and maintenance of the facility" is curiously obscured. It may be recalled that residents are assigned to a work crew during their "intake" interview, even before they are assigned a "primary therapist." The nature of the work obviously supports the operation and maintenance of the facility.

The ordering, obtaining (going to the store), storing, and preparation of all food is the job of the kitchen crew for the benefit of all other residents and staff members who eat some meals in the facility. The kitchen crew even serves coffee to counselors when there is a staff meeting, and sometimes serves meals to counselors in their offices. These latter tasks are performed by request, but the requests are made in a manner that conveys expectation rather than inquiry. While one could conjure an image of such labor as part of a real vocational program, there is little or nothing that suggests that a stint on DTF's kitchen crew might lead to future employment opportunities. A program in food preparation leading to, perhaps, a certificate that would enhance the residents' prospects for hotel or restaurant employment would be the kind envisioned by the funding agency with the expecation that the state office of vocational rehabilitation might contribute funds.

Much of the clerical work is performed by residents in the communications crew. They answer the telephone, duplicate and file the many forms used in the program, keep track of the daily census, and so on. Only those clerical duties that involve confidential information pertaining to residents are outside the purview of the communications department. Residents even participate in the clerical aspects of preparing the annual budget request that is sent to the funding agency.

The maintenance crew performs all tasks that do not absolutely need a skilled craftsperson: the kinds of tasks that even a more than normally 'handy' individual would pay plumbers and electricians to perform. In some cases residents might be formally trained in such skills, in which case they are required to ply their trades on behalf of the facility without pay. The labor of the maintenance crew does not include merely washing and cleaning but also minor carpentry, plastering, window pane repair, and the like.

The laundry crew launders all items that belong to the facility and are not the responsibility of other, individual residents. Individuals are responsible for washing their bedding, which is provided to them, but other items such as curtains are washed by the laundry crew.

It is extremely difficult to measure the amount of time that residents devote to this domestic labor, because there is a good deal of variability, depending on the crew, residents' schedules of appointments outside the facility, and the fact that residents in the highest status category are excused from participation on the work crews. However, if one takes the work of members of the kitchen crew as a norm, residents spend an average of about three hours per day on work that supports the facility. There are varied ways to calculate the value of this labor to DTF. One way would be to figure residents' work according to minimum wage. This would yield a contribution of $10.05 per day. On the other hand, it is reasonable to suppose that minimum-wage labor would not be adequate.[4] Whatever wage one might assign to resident work, it is interesting to compare resident contribution with daily cost of care. The $28.82 daily cost of care, even using minimum wage, could be reduced by $10.00; to look at it another way, without the resident labor contribution, the cost of care would increase by that amount. In fact, if one were to use the rate of pay for similar workers in state- and county-run facilities such as the county hospital, where the average hourly wage is about $9.00, residents could be seen as 'working off' almost all their cost of care. In any case, resident labor is no small contribution to the operation of the facility.

In keeping with the issue of residents' contributions, the issue of food stamps is relevant. All residents who are indigent are eligible to receive food stamps. To my knowledge, the only residents who were not eligible were those who received SSI benefits from the Social Security Administration. During my more than two years of fieldwork, only three residents received SSI benefits for more than one month in the facility. The resident food stamp contribution pays for all food costs except $4,500 per year paid by the funding agency. This $4,500 could well be assigned to the cost of food consumed by staff members so that one can roughly estimate that the residents pay for their own food.

One way in which residents' contribution to the economy of the facility is obscured is by simple assertion. Not infrequently, the program director would tell residents that their crew performance is a treatment issue, and that if their work were really just a matter of task accomplishment, it would be cheaper to hire outside workers. The most remarkable thing about this assertion is that everyone believes it, including the director. Of course, crew performance *is made into* a treatment issue because it is a measure of therapeutic progress. At least for the residents, this means that their crew performance gets translated into moving up and down the resident hierarchy of statuses, and even more immediately it can get translated into weekend passes outside the facility. The latter translation comes about because crew performance, as evaluated by crew chiefs, is a criterion for pass request approval. Therefore, the most immediate reward for labor is increased freedom, a commodity more valuable to residents than money.

Another way labor gets obscured is that it is not 'seen' by regulatory agents. There are two regulatory agencies with which DTF is most concerned: the funding agency and the state licensing agency. During my years of fieldwork, administrators from the funding agency came to the facility on only three occasions. Moreover, these were not evaluations, but guided tours. Visits from the licensing agency are biannual, and they are evaluative. However, investigators paid a great deal of attention to the condition of the physical plant and examined resident files in detail to make sure that all required documents were properly in place. They did not notice the (probably illegal) resident work going on around them.

Another kind of contribution that residents make to the facility is in the form of money. All residents are required to pay a five-dollar monthly fee for services. The intent of this fee is a "symbolic" (i.e., token) investment in treatment. While no one is ever expelled for failure to pay this fee, resident pass requests are denied if they are behind on their "client billing," as it is called. Just as crew performance is made into a treatment issue by connecting it to freedom, so the monthly fee is made into a treatment issue, and its payment is interpreted as a sign of "responsibility" on the part of residents.

The few residents who are in the GP phase of the program are expected to be in school or working. If they are working, their wages are subject to deductions toward their cost of care. This is a requirement imposed by the funding agency, which has devised a complex formula for determining resident contributions. It is so complex that it leaves a great deal of leeway for interpretation. Unlike labor contributions, monetary contributions are treated rather charily by counselors. The most any resident ever paid was twenty-five dollars per week out of net earnings of over one hundred dollars per week; usually the contribution is much less than this. Again, the reason is that such payments are made into treatment issues, not fiscal matters. The issue, again, is one of "responsibility." Showing responsibility means saving toward the day of discharge, and/or making payments on restitution.[5]

Except for GP residents who are working, significant outside sources of income are subtly (and sometimes not so subtly) discouraged. This discouragement applies to such sources as social security payments and unemployment compensation. People who enter the program while receiving social security or unemployment compensation find that seemingly minor obstacles are placed in the path of continuing to receive such funds: letters confirming their residency remain unwritten, appointments are superseded by "treatment issues," and so on. These obstacles were never legally challenged, but the fact remains that no one maintained such sources of income and stayed in the program during the observation period. Moreover, attempts to gain income are discouraged. Residents who attempt to qualify for disability income from the Social Security Administration or the Veterans' Administration are discouraged from doing so. Counselors question their motives and imply that they desire the money only to buy drugs. When residents do apply, requests for information by the relevant government agencies are ignored for months, and when the information is supplied, it tends to disqualify the applicant.

Other outside sources of income are always subject to careful scrutiny. Occasional gifts or loans for pocket money are acceptable as long as they are not very large and come from "positive" family members, or even friends; yet there remains an aura of suspicion. Women are often accused of obtaining goods or money from people characterized as former "tricks."[6] Men who obtain money from women other than wives, sisters, mothers, or "positive" girl friends are suspected of "pimping" the women in question.

With the exception of the small number of people in the GP category, residents are not merely discouraged from gainful employment but denied it. Even for members of GP, who are *allowed* to seek employment, active assistance is conspicuous by its absence. The most common intervention with respect to employment for GP residents is goading and harassment to increase the vigor of their job search. Otherwise, staff involvement in resident employment is limited to referral to a job placement agency.

This inside view of the DTF economy is seemingly paradoxical. On the one hand, residents appear to be exploited by having to work in support of the facility. But to see the economic relations as simple exploitation would be a mistake. When it comes to matters of money, the staff are reluctant to accept contributions from residents, and generally discourage monetary income. Work is viewed as morally good and as a sign of progress in treatment;[7] money is treated with some degree of suspicion, in regard to both its source and its potential for expenditure on drugs. It is necessary to turn to the historical view to grasp the roots of this paradox, if not its resolution.

THE HISTORICAL VIEW

In the conceptual framework of the therapeutic community, DTF is modeled on Daytop, which in turn was modeled on Synanon. Synanon was established within a tradition of utopian communities that rejected many of the values of contemporary, mainstream American society. One of the values that was typically rejected by this tradition was what was perceived as an over-emphasis on wealth, especially as a measure of a person's overall worth. The economy of Synanon was communal. All members contributed according to their abilities, and all contributions went into a common coffer. Since most people who entered Synanon were impoverished, their initial contributions usually took the form of labor. Later, as members gained in trust and stature, they went outside of Synanon to bring in material resources. Sometimes this was in the form of earnings from jobs, but it often included the solicitation of contributions—either money or goods and services. The material resources of Synanon were shared among its members, not exactly equally, but everyone's basic needs were met equally. While some members received more from the common fund, the distribution was based on moral stature, not on the amount of their contributions.

Synanon eschewed government funds, although it accepted private contributions, because government support was believed to have strings attached to it, and Synanon might then have to give up its stance toward the larger American social system. The major difference between Daytop and Synanon was that Daytop was established with money from a government-sponsored research grant, and it has continued to rely on government funding. The founding objective of Daytop was treatment and rehabilitation of drug addicts, whereas the Synanon connection with drug addiction was serendipitous. Synanon was first established as a residential commune; only later did it become apparent that many drug addicts were members and that they were abstaining from drugs. DTF started as a Synanon replicate in 1973, but was specifically aimed at treatment of addicts from its inception. At first, it took some money from government sources, but it also relied on other forms of income, more like Synanon than Daytop. It was only when contin-

ued operation with this kind of fiscal structure became un-
feasible that DTF became completely dependent on government funding. Even so, the program was not financially stable until it was purchased by the present parent social
service agency with its connections to the correctional system. Prior to that time, DTF was run along relatively strict
communal lines. While staff members were paid, they were
all former residents of DTF or a similar therapeutic community. Their dedication to the communal principle was more
important than their salaries. After the purchase, more and
more staff members were outsiders, many of whom were
professional counselors without any addiction or treatment
background themselves.

The professionalization of staff is indicative of the grad-
ual conversion from a utopian commune to a social service
agency. As DTF became more of an agency and less of a
commune, and as it became increasingly dependent on government financing, outside contributions from members
(now residents) became superfluous. The loss of the communal character insofar as material resources were concerned
meant that money gained by residents was not common
property, but remained an individual resource. As such, it
conflicted with the communal principles, which were re-
tained despite changing economic realities. Money in the
hands of residents was viewed as a source of corruption,
either because of the manner by which it was obtained or
because of its potential for the purchase of drugs.

At the same time, work could continue to be part of the
communal economy without any strict accounting of labor
contribution either by quantity or quality. Moreover, the
moral importance of work fit with the general orientation of
the treatment program. The stated treatment objective of
DTF that aims "to modify the resident's attitudes and
values" is partly one of turning residents away from "hustling," crime, and illegal work. In the communal ideology,
work is something that benefits all; it is not a selfish pursuit.
"Hustling" is perceived as eminently selfish and antisocial

and closely connected to drug addiction, criminal careers, and, in general, the "dope fiend" way of life. Work without monetary remuneration is ideal because it can contribute to the common social good without being tainted by the corrupting effects associated with the underground economy of which illegal drugs are a part.

The historical roots of DTF in the communal tradition lead to myopia regarding the economic import of labor. The communitarian ideology evaluates labor primarily as a moralresource, something that contributes to the community. Individual ownership of money, in contrast, is associated with artificial social differentiation, exactly the kind of thing that the communal tradition abhors. Therefore, residents' labor can be a moral and treatment matter, but residents' money partakes of the corrupting association with the "dope fiend" way of life and anti-communitarian forms of social differentiation.

The historical tradition also helps explain why the picture seen clearly from the outside—the actual funding system—remains opaque from the inside. The entire government funding apparatus is viewed as a necessary evil, one that should be kept at arm's length. The objective is to insulate the therapeutic community from the anticipated 'strings' attached to government money. The less government has to do with what goes on inside the facility, the better. In the case of DTF, the program administrator and the parent social service agency as a whole provide this insulating effect. Direct contact with the funding agency is kept to a minimum; most communication takes place between the parent agency and the funding agency, not between DTF and the funding agency. While the program director does get involved in the budget process, and DTF does have to receive written approval from the funding agency to admit new residents, fiscal negotiations take place between the funding agency and the program administrator, not the program director. The director knows about fiscal matters, but is only indirectly responsible for them. This limited involvement, even on the part of the program director, makes the fiscal structure a relatively distant concern for staff members and even more distant for residents.

While this historically rooted disinvolvement with government funding may explain the opacity of economic relations from inside DTF, it does not explain why the internal economy is similarly opaque to the funding administrators. Unraveling that question requires a broader understanding of the political position of public drug treatment in general and the position of the funding agency specifically.

The crucial point seen by neither funding administrators nor participants in DTF is that the fiscal structure is that of public insurance. Public insurance differs from private insurance in a number of ways that affect its administration. The most obvious difference is that private insurance is a business designed to make a profit for its investors; in public insurance, the profit motive is lacking. Public insurance is administered by government; private insurance is conducted through privately owned companies. The biggest difference, although it is often overlooked, is that for public insurance the risk is spread over a much larger population. These differences do not affect the flow of money, but they do affect the way the flow of money is perceived.

The perception on the part of funding administrators is that disability funds are more closely akin to welfare programs than to health and disability insurance. In fact, contracts to service providers are let jointly by the funding agency and the county department of social services. One important result of this welfare view of disability funds is that review of programs is conducted by social service administrators. Programs for disability services are not evaluated according to criteria of treatment, but rather according to demand for services. Adequate programs, in this view, are those that meet the demand.

Among private health and disability insurers, when a claim is presented, it is first reviewed to see that it meets various administrative requirements; it is then reviewed by medical experts who evaluate the actual treatment or service performed. While the first kind of review is conducted by the funding agency, the second is entirely lacking. There is no mechanism for evaluating drug treatment *per se*. As one administrator explained, DTF was established when the funding agency was satisfied with any program that offered drug treatment. Once established, there was no evaluation of the treatment, because it was doing its part in meeting demand. Except for formal and sketchy outlines in the form of program descriptions, the funding administrators do not know the nature of treatment in DTF. The only kinds of checks on the payment of disability money are those that guard against fraud, either intentional or unintentional.

Another implication of the welfare view of disability funding is that recipients of services have to take what they can get. Services are proffered; they are not selected by recipients. While individuals who are privately insured may encounter certain limitations on their choice of medical or rehabilitative care, it is they who make the choice and thereby engender payment by their insurance carrier. This is the way private-pay drug treatment works, but not the way publicly supported drug treatment is perceived. While admission of residents to DTF triggers payments, the financial arrangement is treated by the funding agency and the service providers as strictly between them; the recipient is effectively cut out of the cycle. This makes residents entirely dependent on the system, just as welfare does.

From an even broader view, the contrast between drug treatment and other kinds of medical or rehabilitative treatment has to do with the fact that there is no consensus on standards of drug treatment. What is subject to evaluation is whether demand is being managed. On that issue, there is consensus: it is not. Public disability programs are completely swamped by demand for services. Waiting lists for treatment programs are measured in months, and DTF is no exception. While private insurance payments have caused drug treatment programs to proliferate at an astounding rate, funding administrators see public programs as falling behind at an accelerating rate. As demand outstrips supply, recipients of services have a decreasing say in what kinds of services they receive.

One final viewpoint needs to be brought out. DTF is not merely a treatment facility; it is a facility with close ties to the correctional system. In fact, it would not be wrong to say that it has more in common with carceral establishments than with therapeutic programs. Hence, treatment issues are at least as much issues of control and surveillance as issues of therapy—more so in most respects. Therefore, to evaluate DTF's program from a therapeutic perspective would deny the reality of its objectives of control. From the point of view of the correctional system DTF does exactly what is required of it. When it is lax, functionaries in the correctional system are quick to intervene. Probation officers and bail monitors are familiar with the everyday procedures in the facility (unlike functionaries in the funding system). When the procedures do not result in sufficient control, such functionaries do not hesitate to alert the DTF staff.

The dependence on corrections for recruiting residents means that the correctional system has the kind of prerogatives enjoyed by recipients of services under private insurance. Probation officers, not those treated, make the choice of treatment. Again, residents are cut out of the decision-making cycle, just as they are from the flow of payments. DTF articulates the operation of these two systems—corrections and disability funding. DTF is perhaps the only point of contact between the two systems. Its unique position requires little financial accountability, while its source of funds allows it to resist complete domination by the correctional system.

CHAPTER 5

The Ideology

How do we explain the paradoxical coexistence in a
class society of an ethos of individualism, self-reliance,
and personal achievement along with persistent mediation of the individual's place in society by family ties?
Verena Stolcke (1984: 264)

THE UNIQUE POSITION OF DTF between the disabilities
funding agency and the correctional system insulates
the facility from the vicissitudes of its organizational
environment. One of the important consequences of the in-
sulation is a relative degree of autonomy in its internal everyday affairs. However, there are sources of turbulence that
result in an impression of simmering conflict, always threatening to erupt into overt clashes. This impression comes
partly from the fact that there is not one dominant ideology,
but several contradictory ideologies operating in the day-to-
day drama of life in DTF.

CONTRADICTIONS

The ideology centered on the group conflicts with the ideology that exalts the individual. In addition, there is a contradiction between an ideology that supports and rationalizes

the authoritarian and hierarchical mode of decision-making and an ideological tradition of collective communality. This contradiction is linked to another: while the target of change is the individual, the mode of change is supposed to be collective. That is, treatment is directed at individual residents, but the preferred form of treatment is a group endeavor.

These contradictions are not explicit either in the social interaction within the facility or in the reflections of residents and staff about that interaction. Instead, the contradictions formulated into a synthesized ideology that takes explicit form as "the family."

"The family" is traditional in this facility. Prior to the present administration and ownership of DTF, "family" was even part of the name of the establishment. "Family" is found in "The Philosophy," which all residents recite every morning, and all residents begin their announcement of their daily goals by saying, "Good morning, family." New residents are assigned a more senior resident to be as "big brother" or "big sister" (always a same-gender relationship). Moreover, in "The Philosophy," one finds the diatribe against "mother lovers": "Unconditional: Rewards good and bad behavior. Rejecting: Rejects good and bad behavior. Indifferent: Does not care either way. Vacillating: All these mother lovers combined."

The family concept emerges from assumptions about drug treatment in therapeutic communities. It is assumed that drug addicts are infantile due to some character flaw and that they need to grow up again in a corrective familial setting. In the words of Charles Dederich, the founder of the first therapeutic community, Synanon:

> We have here a climate consisting of a family structure similar in some areas to a primitive tribal structure, which seems to affect individuals on a sub-conscious level. . . . A more or less autocratic family structure appears to be necessary as a preconditioning environment to buy some time for the recovering addict. This time is then used to administer doses of an inner-

directed philosophy such as that outlined in Ralph Waldo Emerson's essay entitled "Self Reliance." If it seems paradoxical that an authoritative environment tends to produce inner-direction, it must be remembered that the inner-directed men of the 19th century, viz., Emerson, Thoreau, Oliver Wendell Holmes, Longfellow, were products of an authoritative family structure. It might also be remembered that intellectual, emotional, and spiritual food fed to the recovering addicts while in the climate is rather carefully selected, as cited above. . . . The autocratic overtone of the family structure demands that the patients or members of the family perform tasks as part of the group. (quoted by Yablonsky, 1965: 56–57)

The "mother-lover" part of "The Philosophy" is directly related to Synanon's conception of the corrective effects of the proper family "climate." That phrase encapsulates a theory about the etiology of the residents' character flaws and consequent drug addiction. The theory is that "the parents of most addicts either contributed to or 'hooked in' to their 'child's' problems." (Yablonsky, 1965: 214). That is, the etiology of drug addiction is constructed according to a social-psychological and developmental-theoretical framework that explains the phenomenon of drug addiction according to personality characteristics of addicts, which are presumed to have been acquired through certain kinds of child rearing practices. These personality characteristics must be broken down and new, ostensibly healthier, ones put in their place.

Note that the means of rehabilitation according to this ideology depend on an *image*—that of the traditional American family of the nineteenth century, which was supposed to have produced such admirable figures as Emerson and Thoreau. These figures, then, are the ideals toward which residents should strive. While I never heard mention of Emerson or Thoreau, the abstract images that they represent are pervasive assumptions in the counselors' discourses on residents and their conduct in the facility.

The familial ideology proposed in Synanon is continually reenacted in DTF. It is not just a silent ideal; it constitutes the very stuff of common, everyday interaction in the facility. It explains, rationalizes, and articulates otherwise contradictory elements of social reality. It provides a framework for interpreting 'what is' (the way things happen), and it also suggests a form for the way things should be—a blueprint for an ideal state of affairs. "The Philosophy" makes this explicit. "The family" is the group that is supposed to be "a mirror" to each member: "Where else but in this common ground can we find such a mirror, here together we can at last appear clearly to ourselves, not as the giant of our dreams nor the dwarf of our fears, but as a human being a part of a whole with a share in its purpose."

Much of the effectiveness of the familial ideology depends on what is not said about it. While references to "family" are fairly frequent and the function of the "family" is outlined in "The Philosophy," the kind of family is never specified. The nineteenth-century autocratic family is definitely not part of conscious, public discourse. Because "family" is left vague and imagistic, idiosyncratic meanings can be read into it. In contrast to the vagueness of the image, the affective tone of the concept is spelled out: the "family" here is supposed to offer security, a safe place to grow and mature, understanding, truth, justice, equality; the tone is warm, positive, and optimistic. The familial aspect of the facility presumably offers a place where residents can express themselves without constraint, where they can be "open and honest."

The family concept explains residents' work as something like household chores. The concept also explains the resident hierarchy according to moral seniority. More senior residents have greater freedom and, to some extent, authority over less senior residents much as older siblings have over younger siblings. Despite gradations among residents based on moral seniority, there is still a basic presumption of equality, which in this case ignores their actual ages, differences in education, previous economic status, practical skills, and so on. Residents who are functionally illiterate, who never earned any income, or never enacted any adult roles (e.g., spouse, parent, provider) are morally equal to those who are otherwise their social betters in such respects. As a whole, residents are in the position of children in a very large family where they are treated and judged according to internal familial standards.

THE CENTRALITY OF THE GROUP

Groups are the principal context for the enactment of the familial ideology. The group is the embodiment of the family concept, and it includes both formal and informal groups: resident meetings, therapy groups, work groups, and the resident population as a whole. The group form is central to all activity in DTF, and it is in groups that ideological discourses are realized.

Alienation and deceit are thought to be definitive characteristics of drug addicts and the "dope fiend" way of life. Therefore, "openness and honesty" are the ideological touchstones of all interactions and relationships. It is, of course, in the group setting that one is supposed to practice this "openness and honesty."

This "openness and honesty" is facilitated by minimizing opportunities for privacy. In contrast to individual therapeutic relationships in the wider society, residents' relationships with their primary therapists are not private. Two of the counselors' offices are on the ground floor and adjacent to common rooms, and they have glass doors. Hearing and seeing what goes on inside these offices is not at all difficult. While the other two offices do not have glass doors, the acoustics allow conversations to be easily overheard. Information about residents is shared among all staff members, and with probation officers, bail monitors, and functionaries of the funding agency. The only interested parties who do not have relatively free access to such information are residents' friends and family members.

The arrangement of space and time militate against privacy. The bedroom areas are divided into four dormitory sections. Each section has three rooms: one with three beds, another with two beds, and one with a single bed. The single bedrooms are reserved for the most senior residents. There is one bathroom for each section. The dormitory sections replicate the social order of the facility; they are a miniature version of the resident hierarchy. Residents are assigned bedroom space by the director, who tries to insure the replication of the moral hierarchy. He also tries to avoid congregating residents homogeneously by age, race, and social background.

Only the most senior residents are allowed to go to their bedrooms for solitude. Residents in IP can earn the "privilege" of being alone in their bedrooms for a few hours a week. With these exceptions, residents are expected to spend their waking hours with other residents in common rooms. Moreover, they are expected to be engaged in "treatment-related" activities with their fellows. Residents who seem to be isolating themselves are adjured to participate—to find someone to talk to, for example. Residents who go to relatively hidden, non-public areas (spaces underneath stairwells, the furnace room, etc.) are treated as rule violators and punished if they are caught. There is always a suspicion that they must be engaged in some nefarious activity; otherwise why would they seek to be alone? In general, solitude arouses suspicion.

In addition to this communal structuring of space and time, group living is reinforced in that residents are expected to keep the group as informed as possible about themselves. Various mechanisms promote such publication. This is one rationale for the IP privilege meeting, in which residents submit their weekly goals to group evaluation and discussion. Requests for visitors or for weekend passes are submitted for group approval. All plans are supposed to be discussed with the group—as large a group as possible. Retrospective evaluation of almost any kind of delict invariably asserts that plans that led to the violation were not discussed beforehand with an appropriate group of residents and staff members. It is through public enunciation of goals, plans, desires, and impulses that deleterious consequences are thought to be avoided.

The ideological character of the requirement for "openness and honesty" is apparent in the sometimes strained logic with which it is applied. Two instances illustrate this.

In one case a very senior resident was discovered to have been smoking in his bedroom—a non-smoking area. This is a fairly common rule violation, usually punished by a twenty-four-hour smoking ban. Perhaps because the individual was so senior and was therefore supposed to be a role model, his punishment was a three-day ban. It is expected that residents will violate such bans, and these violations are overlooked as long as they are not blatant, but in his case the violation resulted in a longer smoking ban. The longer the situation continued, the more counselors exerted pressure on him, so that he finally ended up with a smoking ban and a full restriction of indefinite length (which meant that he lost his seniority).

Since full restrictions usually are applied only in cases of "cardinal" rule violations, its application in this case had to be rationalized. The rationalization was based on his presumed failure to be completely "open and honest." This failure included his re-admission to the facility. The resident was unusual in that his original admission had been completely voluntary, he had never been criminally charged, and DTF had never had any kind of legal 'hold' on him. He had successfully graduated six months before his re-admission, had returned to using heroin, and had sought re-admission on his own. He was told that he had not sufficiently explained his return to drugs following his graduation, implying that his last month or so prior to graduation had somehow contributed to his failure to remain abstinent. His violation of the smoking rule was taken as a sign of this earlier failure, a step on the road to using heroin again. After some time, he finally 'confessed' that in the period immediately preceding his graduation he had "really been out of treatment" in that his commitment to the community in

DTF had dwindled. It was this 'confession' that finally allowed him to get off his restriction and eventually work his way back up the resident hierarchy.

The other illustrative case concerns a resident who did not quite fit in the community. He was one of the few residents with a middle-class background, and he had generally maintained a middle-class lifestyle prior to admission. His crimes were also of a more middle-class type: he had been convicted of obtaining narcotics with fraudulent prescriptions. During his residency there were several residents with more or less middle-class backgrounds, and he tended to associate with them while avoiding interaction with most other residents. His isolation from most of the other residents came from his fear of them. It should be remembered that most residents in DTF are thoroughly criminalized, and he was simply afraid of them for this reason. He was charged with several specific rule violations: eating "snacks" (soda and candy) outside of snack time and without "snacks privileges," keeping these snacking items in his room rather than in the food pantry, and participating in "cliques" (unauthorized resident subgroups).

These rule violations were taken as signs that he was not cooperating with treatment. When a severe restriction did not result in a more "cooperative" attitude on his part, he was expelled from the facility. In this case the expulsion was especially threatening because his probation officer was informed of it before he was, so that he did not have a chance to escape immediate incarceration. As in the previous illustration, the punishment was unusually severe, and it was explained by reference to his failure to be completely "open and honest" about his perceived antisocial tendencies.

In each case, the targeted resident did not quite fit into the group: in the first example, the resident entered voluntarily, and in the second, the resident tended to isolate himself. One way to interpret the requirement for "openness and honesty" is that it is a coded expression for blending into the group and fitting the implicit model for addict-resi-

dents. It is through group discussion that residents are supposed to achieve the appropriate fit.

Although the principle of "openness and honesty" in
group discussion can be applied to any act that leads to undesirable results, it is supposed to be especially efficacious
for "cardinal" rule violations. Not only is it thought that
group discussion prevents such violations, but the rules
themselves promote the group. The first cardinal rule, the
one prohibiting drugs, is believed to function in this way
because drugs are thought to inhibit sociation. Drugs are
believed to encourage selfishness and lead to superficial relationships: a drug user relates to others only in so far as s/he
can "use" them to obtain drugs. Violence is interpreted as
prima facie antisocial behavior, hence the rule against violence or threats.

The other two "cardinal" rules support the group ideal
in more interesting ways. The rule against sex and/or ro-
mance between residents prevents the formation of dyads.
Dyadic bonds tend to imply a reduction of more diffuse social bonds with the group as a whole. What is especially
interesting about this rule is that it is severely enforced
against heterosexuality, but much less strongly enforced
against homosexuality. Only a few incidents of male homosexuality were ever brought to light, and I believe that there
was little homosexual activity among the male residents
other than these publicized incidents. There were only two
occurrences of homosexual acts, and neither was attributed
to drug usage (unlike most incidents of heterosexual activity). In both cases, the acts were interpreted not as romantic,
but as acts of domination of one male resident by another.
In each case the resident who was identified as dominant
was expelled, while his presumably more submissive partner
was punished less severely. Homosexual activity among female residents was never made public, despite the fact that
such activity was more common than it was among the men.

The "cardinal" rule against sex helps contain internally
generated centrifugal tendencies, but the rule that prohibits

disclosure of information outside the facility is aimed at external sources. This rule, too, is differentially applied in that staff members, especially counselors, regularly disclose information about residents to outsiders, while residents are not supposed to do the same. This is the one "cardinal" rule that applies only to residents and not to staff members; the other three rules (drugs, sex, and violence) are enforced with respect to staff members.

Moreover, this rule is the least stringently enforced of the "cardinal" rules. It is tacitly assumed that residents relate experiences to family members, even to the extent of identifying other residents by name. No one seems much troubled by this. The only occasions when this rule became an issue were situations in which one resident believed that another had talked to former associates who had some grudge or were otherwise threatening. In these cases the informing resident was punished for the rule infraction, but not merely because s/he had broken this "cardinal" rule; the punishment was for having contact with "undesirable" kinds of people—people who were assumed to be immersed in the criminal underworld.

Counselors regularly violate this rule as they keep probation officers and the like informed of residents' "progress in treatment." Legally and with respect to standards of professional ethics, counselors' tale carrying is covered by the fact that residents give their written consent. On the other hand, residents really have little choice in the matter since the reason they are in DTF is to persuade such people as probation officers that they are going to be rehabilitated. The nondisclosure rule helps define the contours of the group by exempting counselors. Other staff members, the most relevant being house managers, are expected to adhere to the rule as are the residents. Exempting counselors identifies them as not part of the group. Counselors are participants in the social setting, they are often *in* groups of residents, but they are not *of* the group made up of residents.

While the group is put forth as a community, one that operates according to communal principles, it is hierarchically structured with an authoritarian form of decision making. Hierarchical structure and authoritarian decision making do not necessarily undermine communitarian principles, since many communes have operated with a charismatic and authoritarian leader. In fact, according to Rosabeth Kanter's (1972) historical review of communes in the United States, authoritarian hierarchy has been more the rule than not. However, in almost all cases cited by Kanter, the goal of these communes was social reform. That is, they were directed either at changing society as a whole by establishing an exemplary community or at least at bringing about an alternative way of life within a corrupt society.

The explicit goal of DTF is not social reform, but reform of the persons of addicts. Corruption is thought to dwell in the residents as individuals, although social factors are not completely discounted as contributors. There is still a great difference between DTF and these other communes in that the locus of the perceived problem and the target of change are individuals. This results in ideological strain. The strain is between the ideological valuation of the group, and a similar ideological valuation of the autonomous individual.

The Autonomous Individual

In contrast to the ideology of the group, which has to be constructed and interpreted, the ideology of the autonomous individual is stated quite explicitly in the text of "The Awareness System."

> I am totally responsible for my own behavior. A dependent person lives an ineffective life because a dependent person is not responsible for his own life. I am totally responsible for the consequences of my own behavior, the costs, the benefits, and the intended as well as unintended outcomes. The effective person makes his own decisions, selects his own choices, is accountable to self and others for the consequences and outcomes of his decisions, makes no excuses for his behavior or that of others; respects his own feelings and experiences as

well as the experiences and feelings of others and does not deny himself the right to exist as a unique individual. The effective person shares the world with others: is able to enter into another's "world" and admit others into his/her world. The effective person has no need to pretend that he/she is perfect, and does not pretend that he/she cannot hurt or exists alone. The effective living person takes risk in establishing relationships with others. In therapy "an awareness" is an observation of someone's behavior as appropriate or inappropriate, responsible or irresponsible, effective or ineffective. The proper response to an awareness is "thank you." The dependent person engages in either passive or aggressive behavior because he has found these effective for him in manipulating other people's behavior. When I refuse to be manipulated, the dependent person often lacks an alternative way to communicate his needs to me. He becomes aware that his behavior is ineffective. Acting and communicating assertively is an effective alternative to self defeating behavior that does not work. Assertive, responsible behavior and self management set forth the conditions necessary for effective interpersonal functioning: if I can stand up for my right to feel what I say and say what I feel to be genuine, to have my emotional needs met when interacting with others, to be appropriate in my expression of my needs and wants, then I am assertive. If I own what I say and feel, if I am accountable for what I say and do, then I am responsible. Each member of the core therapy group is expected to learn and to teach the awareness system. The awareness system is a system of effective living that helps me manage and monitor my own behavior. I use the awareness system by: (a) Making me aware of how I feel and making others aware of how I feel; (b) Making others aware of how what they say and do affects me and my reactions to them; (c) Being aware of how what I say and do affects how others react to me; (d) Making others aware that I will accept the consequences of my own behavior; (e) Making others aware of the consequences of their behavior and holding them accountable for it while refusing to accept responsibility for solving their problems when they are capable of doing so themselves. The goal of the awareness system is to help each individual in becoming a whole person.

"The Awareness System" is given to all residents when they are admitted to the facility. They are expected to be familiar with it, and they are told to review it frequently, especially as part of the educational intent of restrictions or other punishments.

The ideology of the autonomous individual is presented in a very condensed and concise form in "The Awareness System," but it is elaborated in the book *Help Yourself to Happiness* by Maxie Maultsby. The book is required reading for all residents who are in the Intermediate Phase of the treatment program at DTF. A weekly class is built around the book, and all IP residents must attend. The class is taught by one of the counselors. One of the class requirements is to outline the entire book, chapter by chapter, each week.

Maxie Maultsby is a protégé of Albert Ellis, who wrote a foreword to this volume and who developed a system of verbal therapy called "Rational Emotive Therapy" (Ellis, 1963). This is a self-help book designed to make people happy by giving them methods for discovering what they 'really' want and applying "rational decision making" for getting it. The principal rhetorical device in this book is example, which makes it especially felicitous for understanding how the ideology of the autonomous individual is applied.

Maultsby explains why there is such great emphasis placed on emotion:

> Remember! An emotional feeling is never mistaken; and it is its own proof. It doesn't make sense, therefore, to look for evidence to prove that an emotional feeling is real or correct. That's like asking yourself for the evidence that you feel a real or correct pain when you stick a burning cigarette to your hand. The feeling is its own proof. (Maultsby, 1975: 183)

"Emotional feelings" are emphasized because they are in immediate contact with the absolute subjectivity of the person. They cannot be mistakes because there are no mediating factors that could be the source for error. The source of error, according to Maultsby, is the mediation of mistaken and/or "irrational" beliefs and attitudes based on those beliefs. Beliefs, which are patterns of thoughts, trigger or direct emotions and mediate between perceptions and emotions. Thoughts are different from emotions, but they regulate them. Moreover, thoughts are dependent on the medium of words. Again, Maultsby:

> First and most important, your words are essentially the same as your thoughts. And that fact is so important for rational self-counseling. . . . Since your words are your thoughts and because the thoughts you believe cause and control both your emotional feelings and your physical actions, that means your *self-control* is the result of your *choice of words*. When you are *neither* lying nor joking, you react *logically* to your own words. Now do you see why it's so important to be as careful when you talk to yourself as it is when you talk to other people? (Maultsby, 1975: 177–178)

Words are crucial in this schema, because they are the embodiment of thoughts that direct core subjectivity in the form of emotions. Thinking is self-talk, silent cogitation using words. Hence, words should accurately reflect objective reality if one is to respond appropriately to it emotionally and physically.

Maultsby maintains that rational self-counseling is effective therapy for drug and alcohol addiction because addicts use drugs to relieve unpleasant emotions caused by irrational beliefs. In the class that uses this book numerous examples are used to illustrate this principle. One of the most common kinds of examples comes in response to a question or a resident's objection to the theory. Residents would say that they feel depressed, sad, lonely, or angry, because they do not have good jobs, comfortable housing, secure family relationships, and so on. The teacher's response follows a format provided by Maultsby:

You got confused because you thought I meant that people only act to get material things like money, etc. Those are just secondary motivations; the single most important factor in human motivation is *emotional feeling*. Money *means* nothing if you *have no* desire for it. It's only because desires are merely emotional urges to act that money gets you to act, if and *only* if, you have the proper emotional feeling or urge (i.e. desire) for money. (Maultsby, 1975: 185)

Such observations are usually followed by applying the principles of "rational decision making" to improve material circumstances. The teacher points out that residents know how to get material things while running lower risks than those entailed by criminal activity. A "rational" approach would involve acquiring job skills, typically through education, so that residents could get better jobs and earn more money. This is followed by a reminder that the residents' behavior has been ineffective in the past. They felt sorry for themselves because they did not have things that they want. They tried to kill the unpleasant feelings with drugs, and they pursued material gain through the high risk business of crime, again feeling sorry for themselves when they got caught.

When residents object to the teacher's explanation by saying that they are at a disadvantage in pursuing their goals in this manner, the teacher answers by pointing out that there are no objective prohibitions against the residents' pursuing the same paths to material gain that law-abiding nonaddicts pursue. The residents merely ("irrationally") *believe* that they cannot do these things.

SOCIAL IDENTITY

The group is the crucible for the conflict between the two contradictory ideologies in DTF. While groups pervade much of the social life in the facility, conflict and contradiction are most clear in the relatively formal therapy groups and meetings. Therapy groups are especially instructive because they have the least explicit structure. While many of these groups are identified with some name that seems to be descriptive—for example, IA seminar, IP group, Women's group—in fact differences in group process among them are paltry.

The process in almost all therapy groups follows the same pattern. One resident (sometimes several, if some collusion is suspected) is singled out to be on an informal 'hot seat.' It is 'informal' because it just seems to happen in every group; there is no explicitly stated plan to follow this pattern. Sometimes the holder of the 'hot seat' is known before the group begins, because it has become general knowledge that someone has committed some offense. Alternatively, the 'hot seat' occupant may be known as a holdover from a preceding group. However, the first part of a therapy group session often is devoted to finding a candidate for the 'hot seat.' Only rarely is there no 'hot seat.'[1] Once someone has been identified as a candidate, s/he is confirmed for the office by assaultive verbal sorties about some serious malfeasance or more minor delict that can be taken as a sign of "lack of progress in treatment." The successful candidate will not be able to deflect such attacks. Once the candidate gains the office there is a general free-for-all attack by other group participants.

In the ensuing flurry of insults, accusations, and ridicule, attackers may inadvertently let slip something about themselves that makes them better candidates for the 'hot seat' than the current occupant, in which case the office is conferred on them. This is never the case when the attacker is a counselor. Assaults may flag during these proceedings, and at such times it is the responsibility of a counselor to add fuel to the fire, or shift the attack to someone else.

Perhaps the most exciting aspect of this group process is that it can happen at any time. That is, residents may be participating in some collective activity that seems far removed from a regular therapy group (for instance, the rational self-counseling class) when some resident suddenly is put on the 'hot seat' without warning.

The rationale for the use of group process to put individual residents on the 'hot seat' is that the only way to cure drug addicts is to break through their "hustles" or "dope fiend bull-shit." In staff meetings this is called breaking down "pathological defenses." The idea is that "dope fiends" have developed ways to protect their "stash"—that is, to protect their supply of drugs, literally, and more metaphorically to defend themselves through deceit, false fronts, and dissimulation. The group, composed of such "dope fiends," brings the therapeutic benefit not only to the person on the 'hot seat' but to those who carry out the attack, because they see how truly "ineffective" their own "jive hustles" are. Therefore, both the target of the attacks and the attackers are thought to be beneficiaries.

A number of typical characteristics are attributed to the "dope fiends." "Dope fiends" are always "running a game," involved in some kind of manipulation to gain hidden ends. They earn their livings non-legally by theft and fraud, or legally through enterprises not thoroughly above-board or legitimate. An example of such a "hustle" is the sale of cosmetics to female clerical workers in large office buildings. As the program construes it, these cosmetics are acquired legitimately, but the "dope fiend" takes them to the office workers and sells them on the spot with a substantial mark-up.

All women are assumed to engage in prostitution, even when it is known that particular women have never been prostitutes. Personal relationships are never "genuine," but always superficial; "dope fiends" do not have friends, only associates of the moment. "Dope fiends" always seek immediate gratification, so their fraudulent practices are always directed toward the next opportunity to "cop" drugs; they seldom engage in the "long con" (a long-term fraud that defers a pay-off) except insofar as their whole way of life is a confidence game.

While there are a few residents who actually fit this image of "dope fiends," there are many who do not fit at all or who do some of the things attributed to "dope fiends," but in other ways are anomalies. A few examples illustrate the variation.

One resident, about twenty years old, grew up in the housing projects of Chicago. All his brothers were either in prison or on their way back to prison. He himself was on probation for burglary. He had never had a regular job and had dropped out of high school. So far, his background would fit the "dope fiend" profile. In conversation, however, one discovers that his aspiration in life is to become a policeman in order to protect people, because in the projects he has seen many people hurt, robbed, even killed by violent criminals. His burglary conviction came about because he saw one of his brothers in the act of committing a burglary, tried to persuade him to give it up, and then was arrested along with his brother when police arrived on the scene. He entered DTF by his own request to his probation officer because he was concerned that his actually moderate use of marijuana and alcohol would lead him into the drug world more deeply.

Another young man has a background similar to the first, but in this case he did live by theft and fraud. He also took money from his girlfriends, who garnered the funds through prostitution; in other words he lived by pimping. But he did not spend most of his money on drugs. In fact, one of his greatest pleasures after a successful burglary, for instance, was to rent evening clothes and a limousine and attend the symphony or ballet.

Information about residents that suggests that they might deviate from the "dope fiend" norm is either ignored, or if it is reported by a resident, it is not believed. The objective of "therapeutic" talk in DTF is to get past what are perceived to be diversions and deceptions in order to get at the "real, jive, dope fiend hustler." Residents who protest to the contrary, unless they somehow adapt themselves to the image of the "dope fiend," will continue to be attacked and accused of not making "progress in treatment." Hence, whether a resident is a "dope fiend" or not, she or he must take on the image before treatment can occur.

While individuality is held up as a valued goal, and a method for an autonomous way of life is explicitly taught in the form of "rational self-counseling," conformity to group norms is demanded of all residents. Moreover, the group itself as a unified entity is also highly valued. The ideology of the group is one of communalism with equality presumed among all members. The group as a community is supposed to promote wholeness, growth, and moral health in opposition to extra-community sources of corruption. Participants in this community have identities as members of the group; in other words, the ideology favors a corporate type of identity.

In contradistinction to the corporate identity of group members, independence is stressed in the ideology of the autonomous individual. Enlightened self-interest based on independent, rational decisions is the credo of this ideology. One cannot help but think of eighteenth-century social philosophy, in which enlightened self-interest is supposed to eventuate in a polity beneficial to all.

The communal ideology presupposes the group from which individual identity is derived, whereas the ideology of the autonomous individual presupposes atomistic persons who, in their collectivity, make up the group. In DTF, both ideologies are fostered and the contradictions between them are not reconciled. However, these contradictions are put together or joined in the formulation of the family of which participants in the facility are supposed to be members. The family combines both ideologies without really articulating them. The result is simmering conflict between residents and staff members, and among residents, who are expected to criticize one another constantly. Affiliations among residents, other than affiliations to the group as a whole, are discouraged if not forbidden.

These contradictory expectations take concrete form in the paradoxical construction of the addict-resident identity. This construction requires residents to adopt a deviant identity in order to be cured of deviance. This process of identity adoption takes on game-like qualities in that the residents must play along in order to avoid possible incarceration if they do not play well. The construction of the addict-resident identity may be a game, but it is one with very real consequences.

How residents and counselors play the game is determined by social, economic, and political discourses. The game is additionally determined *and represented* in the ideology of the program. The ideology describes and prescribes social reality in DTF. It also offers a framework for explaining this reality.

CHAPTER 6

Talk the Talk

A S AT MEETINGS OF ALCOHOLICS ANONYMOUS, coffee
is 'always brewing' at DTF. Although residents and
staff members will refer to coffee as a stimulant
within their respective groups, they never do so with members of the other group. Staff members drink coffee at will,
anywhere and anytime they wish. Residents in the Graduation category can drink coffee anytime they want to, but
they cannot drink it outside the common rooms; they cannot drink it in their bedrooms, for example. Residents in the
Intermediate category, likewise, can drink it at anytime, if
they have earned the "coffee drinking privilege." If they
have not earned the "privilege," they are as restricted in
their coffee drinking as are the residents in the Assessment
category, who can drink it only at mealtimes. The act of
drinking coffee identifies people as members of the different
social strata inside DTF.

Coffee Talk

Coffee is also part of the political economy of the facility.
Residents' food stamps are used to purchase coffee, but the
residents have no say in how it is allocated. The rules of the
program as formulated and enforced by the staff determine

allocation. The minor exception is that residents in the Intermediate category vote on who among their ranks earns
the "coffee drinking privilege." The fact that residents buy
the coffee but do not control its distribution is not acknowledged by anyone in DTF.

Sometimes coffee rules are collectively violated by residents. A group of residents surreptitiously will share a
pitcher of coffee without regard to "privilege" status. Such
secret coffee klatches often take place in locales where no
resident is allowed to drink coffee—for example, in a resident's bedroom or in a staff office in the evening when no
counselors are present. This rather furtive rule violation is
the limit of the residents' collective resistance.

A split among counselors led to a revealing incident.
Two counselors decided that residents were drinking too
much coffee. They supported the claim by pointing to 'coffee nerves,' or excessive jitteriness, exhibited by some residents. They proposed that decaffeinated coffee be served to
avoid what they considered to be the deleterious effects of
caffeine. They based their proposal on two arguments: caffeine presented a general health hazard, and excessive nerv-
ousness produced by caffeine interfered with the treatment
process—that is, residents were too nervous to participate
effectively in treatment. Their proposal became a source of
conflict among the staff because coffee came from one large
brewing urn for the entire facility, so if decaffeinated coffee
were to be brewed, regular coffee would be unavailable to
everyone, staff included. Most of the staff preferred regular
coffee, because they wanted the "buzz."

The implications of the proposal did not become clear
until a general House Meeting including both residents and
counselors convened. During the meeting, issues of health,
alternative beverages such as herbal teas, and treatment-related effects of coffee were talked about, but no one mentioned coffee as a stimulant. Not until one resident did directly refer to enjoying the "high" he got from coffee did
this avoidance become clear. His remark was met by silence,

a 'pregnant pause'; then the talk of the meeting resumed. Ordinarily, any reference to "getting high" by a resident is an occasion for some sort of discourse on the evils of drugs and the resident's "dope fiend" way of thinking. In this coffee meeting, no such response was forthcoming; his comment was ignored by everyone.

After the coffee meeting, it was decided to go with decaffeinated coffee. The two counselors who had started the anti-caffeine movement directed the dietitian to purchase only decaffeinated coffee. However, the resident who was head of the kitchen crew secreted some regular coffee, so that staff and residents who wanted the caffeine could have some. This secreted coffee was treated similarly to a "stash" of illicit drugs: counselors would meet with the head of the kitchen in the pantry, making sure not to be observed, in order to arrange for some regular coffee to be brewed. When this "stash" became depleted, the director (one of the pro-caffeine staff members) authorized the use of petty cash money to purchase more regular coffee. This unusual situation broke down the 'wall of silence' about the drug aspect of coffee as it undermined the otherwise rigid distinctions between staff and residents, and it altered the internal economy of coffee so that program funds (the petty cash) replaced funds coming from residents.

CIGARETTE TALK

In DTF, almost everyone smokes cigarettes. The main rule regarding cigarettes that is a matter of continual conflict is the rule that forbids cigarette exchange. (Actually this is a specific application of the rule that forbids exchange of any goods or services among residents.) The rule is broken frequently, because the custom among residents is that cigarettes are governed by a principle of generalized reciprocity. For the most part, cigarettes are freely "borrowed," and no strict accounting is kept. A resident who has cigarettes gives them to other residents on request, and those residents who do not have cigarettes feel free to request them. One of the reasons for this custom is that residents tend to obtain 'spending money' erratically, so residents' supplies of cigarettes are erratic as well.

The rule forbidding cigarette exchange is never enforced by residents against one another, whereas other cigarette-related rules are enforced. For example, one resident will put another on a "smoking ban" for failing to put away an ashtray. Only counselors enforce the cigarette exchange rule, and they enforce it very selectively. Selective enforcement is freely acknowledged, and both residents and staff members speak about it. Although it is often rationalized by saying that the rule inhibits the formation of "negative contracts," selective enforcement of a rule always reveals the exercise of power. It is when rules are not applied selectively that they take on the cloak of natural laws, but residents and staff debate this rule continually.

During an annual 'retreat' the cigarette exchange rule became a matter for discussion among staff members. The same kinds of arguments were used in discussion of 'drugs,' although the psychotropic effects of tobacco did not come into the matter.[1] Arguments about the effect of cigarettes on health were common, but so were arguments about its association with a "negative" lifestyle, the fact that cigarettes contributed to "negative contracts," and the fact that cigarettes are just another form of addiction that can lead to a return to illicit drug use. In other words, cigarettes were subject to the same kinds of evaluations as those to which, say, heroin is subject, despite the fact that no one claimed that cigarettes are a drug.

When it came down to a final decision about abrogating or retaining the rule against cigarette exchange, all the moral and health arguments were discounted. The staff decided to retain the rule strictly on the basis of the control it afforded counselors over the residents.

While it might seem astonishing that the issue of control was acknowledged so explicitly, it should be remembered that control is thought to be a regular and important function for counselors. In this respect, residents are believed to be people who are "out of control"—especially because they lack self-control. The control function of counselors is supposed to be a temporary measure until residents can "internalize" these controls, thereby leading to growth in their personal autonomy. For the issue at hand, regulating cigarettes was conceived as part of this "internalization" process.

The fact that cigarettes were talked about in the same way as illicit drugs suggests that this commodity (cigarettes, tobacco) remains on the 'edges' of the drug category without any claim of similarity in intrinsic properties. The discussion highlights at least an implicit acknowledgment of the social nature of the definition of 'drugs.'

Aspirin Talk

Aspirin, cold remedies, and even vitamins are kept under lock and key and dispensed to the residents on request; each incident of dispensation is recorded in a log. In part, this is a requirement of the state licensing agency, but the language of their rule calls for all "medications" to be regulated in this way. What constitutes a "medication" is a matter that allows some interpretation on the part of the facility. The fact that vitamins and antacid tablets are subject to the regulation at DTF, but not at some other facilities governed by the same licensing rules, calls forth the question of 'what is a drug?'

Residents have access to these items only through staff members. This means that staff members have to make diagnostic decisions regarding the 'real need' a resident may have for a "medication." Staff members are supposed to judge whether a resident is sick enough to need a cold remedy, an antacid, or an aspirin. There is always a degree of suspicion that residents might "abuse" these products, presumably in the same way they "abused" other 'drugs.'

Occasionally this suspicion is raised to the level of an accusation that some residents are indeed "abusing" such things as aspirin. On several occasions, special "groups" were called by counselors when they decided that certain residents were "abusing" some over-the-counter drugs. During these "groups" the residents' medication logs were held forth as evidence of the "abuse." The accusations of "abuse" did not involve any rule violation. There was no implication that the residents were using the products to "get high." Moreover, no one suggested that "abusing" aspirin, for instance, would lead to a return to using illicit drugs. The main point of attack was that "aspirin abuse" was a sign of a "problem" on the part of the residents. The "problem" was the addictive character trait attributed to the residents.

'Drugs' and 'drug addiction' are defined in DTF not according to extrinsic conditions, but rather according to traits thought to be intrinsic to the residents. For coffee, cigarettes, and over-the-counter remedies, it is interesting to note which substances were not a problem. There was nothing problematic about the pharmacological properties of the "abused" items. There was nothing about the "abuse" that was illicit. However, according to the construction of drug abuse in DTF, it is fully acknowledged that some drug addicts pursue their addictions completely within the law. Therefore, the drug-crime linkage popular among some analysts of the drug scene is not recognized here. What makes for abuse is neither the object (the drug) nor the way it is obtained. Drug abuse is determined by the abuser.

DRUG TALK

Coffee, cigarettes, and aspirin provide a useful counterpoint to the otherwise unproblematic reference to "drugs." Something can be a drug and not be a drug, depending on who is party to the conversation. Something can be treated as a drug although no one believes that it has any drug-like properties. Products that are drugs but not drugs of abuse can become drugs of abuse because of some characteristic of the user. 'Drugs' are not so clear-cut a referential category, even in the circumscribed social setting of DTF.

Things that always count as drugs—alcohol, marijuana, cocaine, heroin, and so on—are objects of reference on numerous occasions in the facility. Typically, the discourses that include them as referents exclude many other discourses. In fact, the different kinds of discourses with reference to drugs are limited to a discourse on "how drugs have ruined my life," which is encouraged among residents as long as they do not dwell on their actual drug experiences, because these would constitute "war stories"—a forbidden manner of discourse. Another, somewhat similar, discourse is a seemingly straightforward account of drug-use history. This narrative is first elicited during the intake interview. It differs from the "how drugs have ruined my life" story in that the drug-use history includes no implications of deleterious consequences. This is more like a chronicle that merely contains types, quantities, and dates of drug use.

More informative than the drug references in these discourses, however, is the omission of references to certain drugs. Information about drugs, their properties, and their effects seems to be assumed. Little significance is attached to the materiality of drugs despite the fact that a wide variety of substances are reflected in residents' drug-use histories, and despite the fact that the program emphasizes education. Note, for instance, the use of educative terms like "seminar" to describe a number of regular occasions of talk. The program requires a surprising amount of reading and writing, especially considering the relatively low overall educational attainments of the majority of residents. Outside lectures on special topics ranging from family dynamics, to personal hygiene, to AIDS, although not frequent, are not unusual either. And yet there is almost no effort made to provide information on the nature of the kinds of drugs the residents use, nothing on psychopharmacology, nothing on the contents of "street drugs," and nothing on "side effects" or other distal effects of these substances. No concerted effort is made to correct misinformation held by residents about drugs.

Another, related, field of drug talk is also missing. Were it not for my own curiosity, I would not have appreciated the great variation in the ways people administer drugs, because no one ever talks about the subject except in a vague, generalized manner. While some ways of consuming drugs do not admit of much creativity—for example, most people swallow pills in the same way—smoking and injection especially seem to vary with the traditions of various drug-using networks in which people participate. For example, some people were using 150 proof rum to prepare cocaine for smoking, while other people were using other kinds of solvents. (The fieldwork was conducted before smokable cocaine became commercially available.)

Drug talk in DTF lacks reference to modes of administration, despite the fact that this is a fairly common topic of conversation among people who use drugs. That is, after all, how people learn the traditions of their drug-using networks; in fact it is how people learn the techniques of consuming drugs. Of course, the reason residents in DTF do not engage in much talk about how to take drugs is that such talk is forbidden.

The only exception to this rule occurs when someone confesses to an incident of drug use. Even here, in the confession that is supposed to be a detailed description, there seems to be little interest in the mechanics of the incident. What kind of drug is of interest. How a person obtained the drug is of interest (especially if it involved some other forbidden act like an unauthorized telephone call); the staff especially want to know if any other resident knew about the incident, because the incident then becomes a drug-using conspiracy with concomitant "negative contracts." What the resident actually did in taking the drug is treated as unimportant.

One of the most glaring omissions in the drug talk in DTF are references to the drug market. Most residents know the drug market only at the level of consumption, but even within this level there can be some variation. For example, one of the residents had been involved with the importation of marijuana, and although he did smoke marijuana, cocaine was the drug that he believed was problematic for him. His knowledge of the cocaine market was limited to immediate sources of supply. Most residents know the market only in terms of immediate supply, and while they would sell drugs, they were by no means regular wholesalers. Even residents whose choice of drugs is mainly ethical pharmaceuticals know something about the illicit drug market, because they often obtain one drug from a pharmacy in order to sell or trade it for another.

Any regular consumer of illicit drugs must know where s/he can obtain them. Because drugs are illegal and because people who sell these substances are erratic in their ability to assure continuous supply, consumers must know a number of different suppliers. Outside DTF, this kind of knowledge is a frequent topic of conversation. Inside DTF, this kind of talk is forbidden. Moreover, there is no attempt to educate residents in the nature of the drug market.

Incidents of drug use occasion exciting discourses and stories, especially when they are performed in "crisis groups." Discourses and stories in which one or several residents are characterized as "dope fiends" or in which a particular act is characterized as a "dope fiend move" are often not limited to "crisis groups," and they often do not include any mention of drugs or incidents of drug use. "Dope fiend move" is almost always a negative characterization and just as often comes from residents as from counselors. It can refer to any undesirable, annoying, or contumacious act. The presupposition is that "dope fiends" always have but one ultimate goal in mind, that of "getting high," and that they are not scrupulous in the means they employ to attain it. Thus, failure to empty an ashtray or put away one's coffee cup is characterized as a "dope fiend" move. The "dope fiend" epithet can be used in the absence of any connection to drugs themselves.

The metaphor 'drugs' cuts through the cultural encyclopaedia in DTF. What makes the metaphor controlling in DTF, as opposed to just metaphorical, is that it restricts the meaning of 'drugs' to the essential character flaw attributed to addicts. The metaphor is limited not because of lack of imagination or because of a situated claim for rhetorical or poetic purposes, but for purposes of social domination.

CEREMONIAL TALK

Ritual and ceremony often have afforded analysts an opportunity to use an explicitly framed event to gain an understanding of social order. Perhaps the most informative ritual in DTF is the morning meeting. It is the one regular and authorized event that usually is attended only by residents. Counselors can attend, but they do so rarely. Therefore, by surface appearance it seems to be a resident-determined activity. It is not, but that makes it all the more instructive. In fact, it raises an interesting question: why do the residents continue to enact it in its traditional, ritual form?

Residents gather in the basement, and the meeting begins at 9:00 AM. One resident, chosen by round in the previous meeting, reads "The Philosophy" out loud. When s/he has completed the reading, each resident, in turn, stands and says, "Good morning, family" and identifies several personal goals for the day. The group responds to each resident by saying, "Good goals." "In-depths" follow in which at least two residents (one in Assessment and one in the Intermediate category) stand in front of each co-category member and offer opinions about the other person's character and behavior. Then there is a general, usually fairly brief discussion of house business, announcements, and the like. The meeting ends with all residents standing in a circle with their hands joined to recite the "Serenity Prayer."

The sequence juxtaposes the two ideologies of the facility: particularistic communal solidarity and universalistic individualism. "The Philosophy," which is a statement of the communal, is followed by residents standing singly and telling personal goals, to which there is a communal response. Then the "in-depths" are again individualized, and they are followed by a mixed event (the house business) while the finale is again the communal prayer. In outline the sequence looks like this:

Communal//Individual//Communal//Individual//Mixed//Communal

The sequence is bracketed by the communal: all that occurs, occurs within the community, or "family." The structure has its effects on the residents; it communicates to participants, but they do not talk about it.

There is another alternation in the morning meeting in addition to that of Communal//Individual. This second opposition is Active//Passive. "The Philosophy" and the "Serenity Prayer" both address an absent, superordinate agent. In "The Philosophy" the residents say, "We share in this belief that if *you* treat *us*"; and in the prayer, the residents say, "*God* grant *us*." Thus within two main, bracketing statements of communalism, there is an opposition set up between an "us" and an external agent. In contrast, in the episodes of individualism, residents address each other. Expressions of individualism are kept within the group, while expressions of communalism oppose the group to an outside object. Also noteworthy is the fact that the group is defined as passive with respect to the outside agency and active with respect to its members: "a human being [is] a part of a whole. . . . In this ground we can each take root and grow, not alone anymore as in death." Individuals get their personhood from the group, but the group as a whole is "treated" or "granted" by something outside itself.

The oppositions of communal versus individual and active versus passive are reiterated in each element of the ritual. An example is the "in-depths," which are always carried out between two residents of the same category. No rationale for this procedure is offered; it is 'customary.' However, recently admitted residents are given rationales about the purpose of "in-depths." They are supposed to be an exemplary instance of the norms of "openness and honesty."

The recipient of an "in-depth" remains silent during the discourse and shakes the speaker's hand; then the speaker moves on to the next recipient. The reason given is that "in-depths" are not meant to build relationships, but to provide an opportunity for free expression of thoughts and feelings on the part of the speaker. Although an "in-depth" is addressed to one particular resident, it is supposed to have validity for all.

As they are practiced in DTF, "in-depths" are routinized and formulaic, and there are certain, 'approved' topics for the discourse. The speaker can comment on how people do their work crew jobs, whether other residents are or are not making "progress" in the program (usually as certified by evidence of approval or disapproval from counselors), what kinds of attitudes other residents have been displaying (e.g., frivolous or serious, sad or happy, angry or calm), or any other observations that are obvious to everyone. There is little that is in depth about "in-depths."

Observations expressed during "in-depths" are programmatically conventionalized; they are the same kinds of comments that one finds in the "privilege meeting." They do not so much reflect personal attitudes and opinions as reflect how others are playing the treatment game and, obversely, a display on the part of the speaker of how well s/he can play that game.

The display of skill is not to be taken lightly, because all residents have a lot riding on it. It may be a game, but it is a very serious game; losing it could mean going to prison. "In-depths" provide a rehearsal for the rest of the day. When counselors are present, the "in-depths" are even more conventionalized than usual.[2]

Nor is the skill one that is easily acquired. The key to the treatment game in DTF is to appear to act ingenuously while shrewdly pursuing strategies to increase one's moral account, often at the expense of other residents. At the same time, one cannot afford to offend other residents; one has to present oneself as no serious threat to other residents' strategies. "In-depths" provide an opportunity to affirm this to the group. For the speaker, they are a way to assure other residents of predictability.

When a small group of residents tried to eliminate the more ritualistic parts of the meeting, they were moved to this project because they had been converted to a belief in the effectiveness of a rational approach to living promulgated in the rational self-counseling class. They believed that the morning meeting rituals were irrational. They convinced a majority of other residents to dispense with the ritual practices, but a few days later, the residents voted to reinstate the practices. When I asked the residents who voted in favor of reinstatement why they wanted to return to the traditional form, they told me that the ceremonies made them feel more comfortable and gave them a sense of "real family."

The framing of the morning meeting ritual and its formal content (i.e., the form of "The Philosophy," the rules for "in-depths," and the like) are not something that the residents have invented or reinvent every morning. This is not in any sense a ritual rooted in the group; it is an imposed ritual. Historically, it is derived from the original therapeutic community, Synanon.

However, in Synanon, there could be a higher level of social integration achieved in part through ritual enactments. Residents there could progress to leadership within the community. Centrifugal social forces did not disrupt the integrity of Synanon; instead they spawned replications of it, of which DTF is a third-generation example. Therefore, in Synanon the subordinated group of junior residents was, in fact, absorbed into a system. Neither of these outcomes is possible in DTF. In DTF, residents cannot aspire to leadership positions. When they graduate from the program, they leave it; they do not become counselors. In addition, centrifugal forces cannot lead to the establishment of replicas of DTF because at the present time residential treatment establishments are started by treatment professionals and people in the social services industry, not by cured drug addicts. Therefore contradictions are reiterated, not resolved. The morning meeting ritual is an enactment of this reiteration. There is no higher level of integration expressed at the end of the ritual.

Another force that acts against achieving greater social integration is that social integration is not the goal of the program. In fact, steps are taken by the counselors to stop greater social integration. The goal of the program is to produce reformed drug addicts, so the only higher level of integration that is promoted is that of an individual's personality rather than that of the group.

Counselors are taken to be the interpreters of the ritual by both the residents and the counselors themselves. The counselors authorize—lend significance and authority to—the enactment of the ritual. The irony of this viewpoint is that the counselors are perceived as the carriers of the ritual tradition as well as the authorizing agents of it. In fact, however, the counselors learn the ritual tradition from the residents' enactment of it; they then enforce the tradition among the residents. This process is the same as that found with respect to the rules of the program. The counselors learn most of them from observing residents but are automatically the authority for those rules.

In DTF, clinging to those forms that reinforce subordination cannot be interpreted simply. The residents' motivation should not be understood merely as an infantile wish to return to parental authority, although such motivations probably play a part in their emotional attachment to the idea of "family." The family form also must be understood as an attempt at resistance to institutional domination through attempts to carve out new identities.

DISCOURSES OF IDENTITY

According to authorized discourses in DTF, there are two main opposing identities for participants: residents and staff. While there is some differentiation within the two categories, members of each are organized around a central, defining *type*. For the staff, this type is that of the counselors. Differentiation is a matter of slight divergence from the type identity. Thus, house managers, the dietitian, the teacher, and the consulting psychologist are recognized as different from counselors, but their position with respect to residents is determined by the opposition between residents and counselors.

In a similar manner, differences among residents are recognized, but these differences are variations of a single identity and positional type, that of the addict-resident. Formal, programmatic differentiation of this type identity is the three-step set of resident categories (Assessment, Intermediate, and Graduation). These are ordered along a continuum regulated by the moral economy and reflecting at one end (those in Assessment) as more addict than resident, at the other end (those in Graduation), more resident than addict, while the Intermediates are what the sobriquet suggests.

Other differentiations recognized among residents can be arranged along a continuum of acknowledgment. For example, residents' respective "drug of choice" is recognized as a differentiator, but this recognition leads to little difference in treatment. The degree of acknowledgment given to race, class, and gender (arguably, the three most important identity categories in American society) seems determined by the degree of 'fit' between them and the addict-resident identity.

GENDER TALK

In very broad terms, gender differences are of three kinds: those that are publicly acknowledged, those that are denied, and those that are repressively ignored.

At one time, the head of the kitchen crew was a woman, and the head of the maintenance crew was a man. Both reported difficulties in managing their crew members: neither could get their crews to follow directions without continuous struggles over authority and power. When the male head of the maintenance crew consulted with counselors about his problem, he was advised and instructed in terms that stressed efficient performance. He was told that his position as crew chief was therapeutic because it was providing him training for future occupational roles. Differences, disputes, and rebelliousness on the part of his crew members were attributed to errors in leadership decisions. He was advised to organize tasks differently, and assign different people to them. He was assured that by means of these organizational adjustments, his difficulties would end. In contrast, the woman who was head of the kitchen was told that her difficulties arose from emotionally based, antagonistic personal relationships with her crew members. She was advised to find a way to reconcile these interpersonal tensions, and assured that if she were successful, her management problems would be solved.

Lest it be thought that they are limited to management positions, these gendered constructs are also observable at the level of task performance where no leadership is involved. For example, during staff meetings it is not uncommon for a resident to serve coffee to the meeting's participants. When men serve, they occasionally take the opportunity to engage in mild satire by exaggeratedly acting as butlers or restaurant waiters—a napkin folded over the forearm, requesting staff members for "their order," and so on. These exaggerated performances are comic commentaries on the role as they see it—that is, as performances of occupational tasks—and this viewpoint is reinforced by the staff, who 'appreciate' the performance. In marked contrast is the manner in which women serve. They act as hostesses, as if they were serving coffee to guests in their homes. Again, the performance is 'appreciated' by all. It is possible to infer an opposition between what might be called domestic work and public work.

A similar gendering occurs in regard to space in the facility. The men's dormitories are not very different from the common areas of the facility; female space is marked and restricted to the women's dormitory. Moreover, the signs of these respective spaces follow a gendered code. Male space (i.e., most of the facility) is functional, even spartan. There are few items of personal identification or what might be called 'homey, creature comforts.' For instance, while male residents will put up posters on the walls of their bedroom areas, bring in radios, record players, televisions, in one case even a parrot in a cage, these personal items are limited to the immediate space around their beds. Women extend their efforts differently and more widely. In addition to personal items like those of the male residents, female residents also hang curtains and draperies, erect room dividers, and employ bedspreads. Moreover, women modify the entire dormitory section by using toilet seat and tank covers and bringing in small rugs and other domestic furnishings.

Such 'homey' touches are not only lacking in the male dormitories; they are lacking in the rest of the facility. It looks 'institutional.' Except in the television room, there are no rugs or curtains. Even in that room, where furnishings are somewhat more home-like, the upholstered furniture is notably functional and made for rough wear. The furnishings of the other two large common rooms are definitively 'institutional.' The tables are formica-topped with steel legs, and the chairs are of the folding kind or molded plastic and steel.

This gender-based coding of space is also reflected in some social organization related to space. The women's dormitory is treated by the female residents as something of a haven, retreat, and "backstage" (Goffman, 1959) area. When there are three or fewer women, they do not have a dormitory section but are assigned to the bedrooms on the ground floor. At such times, the women complain of feeling isolated and express a wish for an increase in the female census so that they might feel more support.

In keeping with this authorized organization of space, there is an incipient feminine subculture among the female residents, which is made possible by the women's dormitory. With the availability of this physically bounded area, women perceive themselves as a group embedded in a male, therefore, alien, even hostile environment. There is a certain sense of solidarity. Women 'patrol' the dormitory to keep male residents out of it. They use the staff office adjacent to it for diffuse socializing, and for preparing themselves for more 'public' appearances in the common rooms; the room becomes a place for adjusting one's clothes, arranging one's hair, or applying cosmetics.

This office also serves as a sort of 'drawing room' where women can meet with individual male residents, as long as this incipient community of women perceive the man's intentions to be within the bounds of propriety. In such cases, the women validate such tête-à-têtes by giving the interlocutors some privacy. However, if the collectivity of women assess the man as predatory, his presence in the office calls forth a constant stream of interruptions. A similar practice is carried out beyond the confines of the dormitory as women position themselves into dialogues between a male and female resident to affirm women's solidarity against aggressive male residents.

The foregoing description of an incipient feminine subculture begins to look like a base of solidarity that could lead to resistance against absorption into the program. However, this development is limited to those cultural qualities that fit with implicit (i.e., not publicly stated or otherwise symbolized) program goals. An unstated, but important, goal of the program is to domesticate the female residents. Treatment plans for women are always directed toward making them 'good homemakers' and mothers. It is fairly common to find housekeeping skills as a part of their treatment plans, whereas this is never the case for men. If

women have children, regardless of their present relationship with them or their attitudes about the relationship, the
treatment plan always includes maternal functions as a goal.
Parenting usually is not addressed for male residents. Therefore, the domestication of space, the more domestic manner
of women's work in the facility, even the incipient subculture, are permitted or even encouraged because these phe-
nomena fit with the goal of domestication. In other respects,
women are set against one another, solidarity is interrupted,
and subordination of women to men is promoted.

Nowhere is this more evident than in regard to sexuality.
Program objectives are aimed at channeling women's sexual
interests to those that support home and family. Resident
women are perceived as "dope fiend whoes" (Cleckner,
1982) who have devoted their sexuality to "hustles"—
mainly, prostitution but also other 'women's crimes' such as
shoplifting and sexually tinged confidence games. The program tries to get women to direct their sexual and affection-
ate energies to homemaking and raising children. All female
residents are presumed to have engaged in prostitution.
They are explicitly and publicly labeled "whores" by counselors, and "dope fiend" moves are complemented by
"whorish" moves in the case of women. All women carry as
part of their identities in DTF a presumption of prostitution,
even those women who have never engaged in prostitution.
In contrast, men who have engaged in prostitution are not
called "whores."

While the rule against sexual or romantic conduct applies equally to men and women, the essence of women's
sexuality is treated and constructed differently. In order for
men to be perceived as violating the rule, they must take
overt sexual or romantic[3] action; women only have to be
alluring. While all residents' sexuality is under surveillance,
that of women is scrutinized more intensively as their actions and demeanor are thought to be dangerously seductive. A wide range of women's behavior is so interpreted:
their dress, the way they sit or walk, their voice inflection;

all appearances can be taken as signs of women's inherent concupiscence. The accusations leveled at Sheryl, described in Chapter 2, are by no means exceptional.

For women, but hardly ever for men, this surveillance extends outside the facility. Women's outside relationships are publicly explored for signs of prostitution. Men who cannot be identified clearly as belonging to some kinship category are suspected of being prostitution customers. Favors, cigarettes, small amounts of spending money, even professional services that appear to be more than ordinarily liberal (e.g., a public defender who seems more than usually concerned with a female resident's case) are all suspicious signs. And the burden of proof is on the woman that her relationship with a man is not one of prostitution. Women are assumed to be objects of men's desire, so their sexuality is confounded with their gender. No matter how rigidly they monitor what they do, how they carry themselves, their facial expressions, and so on, their perfidious feminine sexuality lurks beneath the surface.

What is more, female counselors are expected to lead the surveillance of resident women's sexuality. They are the prime investigators and lead the most probing interrogations. In fact, the counselors live up to this expectation so that, for example, the "women's group" tended to be guided mainly by the goal of analyzing the sexual lives, history, and general behavior of the women in order to identify sexual "misconduct." Therefore, any chance of extending some slight degree of solidarity among women across resident-staff lines was undermined before it could begin.

With all this attention given to women's sexuality and their relationships with men, no notice is taken of a very common phenomenon related to the women's pattern of drug use. Although there were exceptions, women's access to drugs was usually through men; it was men who actually obtained the drugs. One of the exceptions was that women who used phoney prescriptions were as likely to "bust the script" (use the prescription) themselves as to receive the drugs so obtained from a man. Men usually obtained the drugs even when they used the women's money to purchase them, so that the drugs still became a "gift" on the part of the man. This was explained by one of the women in a group. Using an example unrelated to drugs to make the point most effectively, she recalled that after her release from jail, she had been picked up by her "man," who took her shopping for clothes to help make her feel better. He bought her several hundred dollars' worth of clothing, and it was not until afterwards that she realized that he was using her money to make the purchases. She specifically related this incident to the way she and other women received drugs from men.

That men "give" women drugs is officially recognized in public discussions in DTF only insofar as it can be related to prostitution-like relationships. It is not viewed as significant in women's drug use pattern *per se*. In other words, this rather common fact is not seen as relevant to women's "dope fiend" ways, which are understood in the same way as those of men.

Race Talk

While gender is subject to variable degrees of acknowledgment and repression, race tends to be subject to blanket repression. When it arises as a topic for discussion, it is treated in a negative manner. For instance, race is a consideration in room and dormitory assignments, where the objective is to avoid racially homogeneous dormitory sections and even out three-person bedrooms. Suggestions by residents that there may be some racially specific interests are analyzed and undermined by counselors. Counselors act as if they have been charged to establish a 'colorless' society in DTF.

Judging from public conversations, counselors seem to be successful in this vocation. A striking but typical example is an interchange between a black resident and a white resident in a group discussion I was directing. The two residents in question had become friendly. In the group, I raised the issue of inter-racial couples.[4] The white resident informed his friend and the group at large that he had very strong feelings against the idea. He elaborated by saying that he based his objection on his belief in the inherent racial inferiority of black people. His friend, who was black, was disturbed by these statements. But what is most revealing is that the two had participated together in numerous groups that are supposed to explore the most intense and intimate details of residents' lives, their beliefs, values, and attitudes. They had, on several occasions, exchanged "in-depths" and had otherwise been engaged in the culture of "openness and honesty" of DTF. Despite all of this, the black resident had no idea of the racial views of his white friend.

Race as a topic for public talk may be successfully repressed in DTF, but that does not mean that discourses of race do not affect people in displaced and disguised forms. There is a vague and very general recognition that there exists such a phenomenon as "black culture" in this country, although no particulars are ever publicly attached to this recognition. One of the black counselors, however, was noted for being more demanding of black residents than of white residents. In a staff meeting, while speaking about a particular case, this counselor mentioned in passing[5] that, "of course, stealing is approved among black people." While this counselor was the sole black counselor at the time, one of the house managers at the meeting was black. He pointed out to the counselor in question that stealing was not a positive value where he had grown up. Had the house manager not been present, the counselor's remark would have gone unquestioned because of the pervasive repression about race in the facility.

Practices relating to pass and visit requests reveal displaced and disguised discourses on race as well. Generally speaking, pass and visit requests have to involve either family members or "positive" friends. It is not uncommon among black residents to make a request involving a "cousin" who is, in fact, fictive kin—that is, not related by descent or marriage. Instead, the individual is part of a resident's extended helping network (e.g., Miller, 1986; Stack, 1974; and Valentine, 1978). First, such requests by black residents are almost always questioned, while similar requests from white residents are never questioned. Second, these "cousin" requests by black residents are usually denied because the "cousins" are discovered to be not "cousins" after all. Various white residents are members of ethnic groups that also employ fictive kinship categories, but since these are never questioned by counselors, the usage remains hidden.

Related to the fictive kin issue is a presumption of guilt when it comes to outside acquaintances of black residents. That is, black acquaintances of black residents are *always* assumed to be part of the resident's drug-using or criminal network. Their bona fides must be established by the resident by demonstrating some familial, professional, or otherwise acceptable basis for the relationship. This is not to say that acquaintances of white residents are not subject to similar scrutiny; often they are. The difference is that acquaintances of black residents are *always* questioned.

An important part of the ideology of DTF is the value of egalitarianism, and a significant feature of this egalitarian value is an official stand against racism. However, this official expression represses, displaces, and distorts racially based discourses that operate in relative silence but clearly have their effects.

TALK ABOUT CLASS

A condition similar to that of race applies to class. A strong egalitarianism denies the significance of class even while class-related discourses have a significant impact on the lives

of the residents. Of the over two hundred residents who passed through the facility while I was there, only about half a
dozen had backgrounds that qualified as middle class. All
the rest came from lower-class backgrounds, either lower
working-class or underclass. Probably the most significant
aspect of class in DTF is that its significance is never acknowledged.

The relative homogeneity of the class backgrounds of the
residents means that interactions within the facility do not
reveal class discourse as an important factor; there is no
basis for comparison, so everyone 'looks' the same. This
equality of appearance supports the ideology of egalitarianism. The homogeneity and egalitarianism hide some important facts from residents.

One of these hidden, actually repressed, facts is that the
goals of the treatment program are at some variance with
those of the residents. For the most part, the residents aspire
to a materially secure way of life. The program claims to
"cure" them of drug addiction and crime. Partly due to the
wishful hopes of the residents, and partly as a result of pur-
veying the *Help Yourself to Happiness* approach to life,
there is an implicit expectation of improvement in material
life to be gained from the program. What is conveyed is an
imagistic, vague, one might say iconic belief that residents
can move into the middle class if they are successful in DTF.
This belief is shared by both residents and counselors.

Of course, lack of drug addiction and crime is no guar-
antee of upward class mobility. In fact, it probably has
nothing to do with class mobility. It is not even a prerequisite for upward mobility, although this prerequisite idea is
explicitly expounded in DTF. It goes something like this:
"Stop using drugs and committing crimes, then you will be
able to get a good job if you are a responsible person, and
then you will be on the way to achieving 'the good life.'"
One of the few ways in which this discourse has any validity
at all is no longer much of a reality for the residents. At one
time and in a more Synanon-like program, the residents

could have had some reasonable expectation that, if they 'kept their noses clean,' they could become drug counselors. At the present time, cured drug addicts have no better chance of becoming drug counselors than anyone else, which means, in effect, that their chances are actually worse because they are competing with people who have middle-class advantages in their favor.

Another way in which class is silently significant does not pertain to the overall class structure of American society, but rather to the position of residents in DTF and its parallels with their positions in the drug market. Residents are passive consumers of the services provided by DTF. This passivity and economic dependency are explained to them as reflections of their own characters rather than matters of social and economic structures that govern the entire program. Material interests in the program and its operations are denied to the residents: they are dealt with as unquestioning consumers.

The same holds true for their position in the drug market, where they are consumers who have no material interests in the overall economic structure. They buy what is available—that is, what is marketed to them. Despite the fact that consumers provide the essential economic foundation, the significance of that position is utterly obscure. The occlusion of the position of consumers, of illicit drugs especially, is supported by law enforcement, which helps insure that consumers are isolated into very small networks. In fact, at the level of consumption the illicit drug market resembles the cadre of an illegal political party organized into cells. The notion behind the cellular organization is that, if a member is caught, she or he can subvert only a limited section of the party or movement as a whole. A similar rationale could be applied to the consumer-level structure of the drug market, the effect of which is to maintain docile and easily exploitable consumers and low level retailers.

This particular feature of class can, of course, be expanded to apply to the overall class structure of American society. The residents' position in DTF also parallels the position toward which their treatment and rehabilitation aims—workers and consumers who do not 'make waves.' Whether one applies the internal class system of DTF to the drug market or to the overall American class structure, the point is that the DTF experience for residents reiterates their material position outside of the facility. Moreover, it connects material dependency and passivity with communalism through the construction of the addict-resident identity. The class position of residents in DTF obscures their relationship to 'the means of production' (i.e., the fiscal workings of the facility) as noted in Chapter 4. The addict-resident identity is essential in this occlusion because it is through the ideological construction of the identity that material relations are converted into matters of personality defects. This process is merged with communalism as potentially alternative identities—those that could be built up around gender, race, and/or class—are repressed and otherwise manipulated to fit in with an homogeneous identity *type*, the addict-resident. Therefore, communalism and group membership is made into a dependent and passive position, and potentially liberating discourses among residents are interrupted.

Interrupting Oppositional Discourses

Gender, race, and class offer potential bases for alternative identities around which oppositional discourses could be articulated and oppositional movement could be organized. However, these alternative identities are not the only potential sources of opposition.

The history of a "clique" illustrates the pattern. A group of six or eight residents (the number is not exact because membership was loosely defined) began to coalesce around getting together in the basement for coffee and informal conversation during the period between breakfast and the morning meeting. This opportunity for diffuse socializing for ten or fifteen minutes away from the eyes of staff led them to seek reenactments of the situation at other times and places. They sought other out-of-the-way places during 'in-between' times of the day. After this had been going on for perhaps two weeks, staff members began to notice that the same group of people usually could be found together.

This gave immediate rise to suspicion. Not only were these residents probably engaging in such rule violations as pouring coffee for one another and exchanging cigarettes, but they were interacting in a jocular manner. Indeed, the person who was the cynosure of the group, at least in the eyes of an outside observer, was a kind of 'class clown.' This character trait had been noted by his "primary therapist" when she made her presentation of his case in a staff meeting. At that time, and subsequently, the counselors devoted some time to analyzing this character trait, relating it to inferred insecurity on his part and connecting that, in turn, to his drug addiction and what they perceived as his flamboyant lifestyle. The consulting psychologist suggested that his outward pose as a comedian hid a deep depression. There was little mystery to his depression and insecurity: he was facing very serious charges of assault because he had been convicted of a shooting. Moreover, he had been involved in drug smuggling and feared that his associates in this enterprise were worried that he would "snitch" on them to avoid going to prison for the shooting. Moreover, this depression and insecurity were not especially "hidden," as any serious conversation with him would have revealed. After several counselors said that they had noticed this group's gatherings, the counselors decided to call together the "clique" in order to investigate what was going on. The director and several counselors confronted the "clique." Of course, everyone in the "clique" denied any serious wrong doing— that is, no drugs or sex. Since the counselors could not unearth any incriminating delicts, they proceeded to interrogate the members of the "clique" individually, and finally had each of them write "cop-out" essays. These essays are written under supervision. Each resident is supposed to describe any rule violations that he or she may have committed and any rule violations anyone else may have committed. The rationale for this procedure is that since no resident knows what the others are writing, each will exercise "openness and honesty," because if a resident does not admit to a violation that someone else identifies, the consequences increase in severity even for very minor infractions.

Even after employing these investigatory procedures, the counselors still could not identify a serious conspiracy. The next step, therefore, was to call a "crisis group" of all the residents in the facility. Inasmuch as "crisis groups" are occasions when residents can make major gains or sustain large losses in their standing in the moral economy, the groups are supposed to be especially efficacious for "open and honest" confrontations. That is why therapy groups in general and "crisis groups" in particular are such a mainstay of the treatment program.

As a result of the "crisis group," the "clique," collectively and individually, was accused of not taking treatment seriously, so that each member of the "clique" was required to write a justification for why they should be allowed to remain in the program. Their probation officers and/or bail monitors were notified that they were close to expulsion. The 'class clown' was a particular target, and he was placed on an indefinite, full restriction. All members of the "clique" were placed on "communication bans" with each other so that they could not speak to one another or communicate in any other way except in authorized therapy groups. It also meant that if they were observed in close proximity to one another, it could be assumed that they were breaking the "communication ban" and thus be subject to further punishment—in this case probably expulsion.

While the "clique" was accused of showing insufficient gravity in their approach to treatment, the specific behavioral breach was "excessive laughter." In other words, no major conspiracy was ever uncovered. When similar procedures are followed with other "cliques," a drug and/or sex conspiracy is sometimes revealed, but these are absent just as often. In either case, the nascent subgroup is disrupted and a potentially oppositional discourse is interrupted and repressed.

The "communications ban" employed against members of a "clique" is a highly repressive measure, and it is important to note that it is used not only against identified "cliques." Its use is quite liberal, often applied to pairs of residents who seem to be getting too 'chummy,' but against whom no more serious accusation can be established.

The construction of the addict-resident identity and the establishment of homogeneous, passive, and dependent communalism do not proceed unopposed in DTF. Other sources of collective opposition occur, but they too are repressed. There is nothing vague, mentalistic, or mystical about this repression. It takes the form of concrete, observable acts carried out mainly by counselors.

Despite rules that inhibit unauthorized sociality among residents—not the least of which is the rule that forbids material exchange—residents do manage to form subgroups. These are not grounded in alternative social identities, but tend to form among residents who get along with each other. On the face of it, one would think that such subgroups would not be perceived as challenging the social order of the facility, but this is not the case. Based on the vehemence of staff response, such groups appear to be major subversive movements. When such groups come to the attention of counselors, they are labeled "cliques," and strong measures are undertaken to disrupt them. The rationale for these 'counterinsurgency' measures is the central idea of "negative contracts."

CHAPTER 7

Conclusion

In the space of one hundred and seventy-six years the
Lower Mississippi has shortened itself by two hundred
and forty-two miles. That is an average of a trifle over
one mile and a third per year. Therefore, any calm person, who is not blind or idiotic, can see that in the Old
Oolitic Silurian period, just over a million years ago
next November, the Lower Mississippi was upward of
one million three hundred thousand miles long, and
stuck out over the Gulf of Mexico like a fishing-rod.
And by the same token any person can see that seven
hundred and forty-two years from now the Lower Mississippi will be only a mile and three-quarters long, and
Cairo and New Orleans will have joined their streets
together, and be plodding comfortably along under a
single mayor and a mutual board of aldermen. There is
something fascinating about science. One gets such
wholesale returns of conjecture out of such a trifling
investment in fact.

Mark Twain

ANYONE WHO OBSERVES the day-to-day affairs of DTF
will conclude that the lives of the residents are tightly
controlled. It will also be clear that this control is

achieved with the residents' consent, perhaps not entirely willing consent, but consent nonetheless. A somewhat closer examination reveals that the residents have created ways to resist this control. Yet these acts of resistance, rather than disrupting domination, seem to affirm it all the more. The fact that the residents resist implies that they are by no means completely mystified by the power that keeps them subordinated, nor blind to the fact that their subordination requires their consent. If residents recognize their common plight, why do they put up with it?

HEGEMONY

Two possible answers present themselves. One answer is that subordinated groups in fact do not set out to make revolutions or formulate counter-hegemonic discourses. Instead, resistances are directed at particular, perceived injustices. This is the answer that James Scott (1985) gives in regard to Malaysian peasants. From his point of view, hegemony is conceived as that which demarcates the arena for social conflict.

In contrast, the other answer is that those who are subordinated have misrecognized the situation; consequently their acts of resistance are misdirected. Pierre Bourdieu (1977) argues in favor of this latter answer on theoretical grounds, and Paul Willis (1981) takes this point of view in his study of British working-class youth. Hegemony here is more than just the rules and boundaries for conflict; it is the regime of truth or what counts as truth. What is at stake in counter-hegemonic discourses from this perspective is not how social battles are to be fought, but rather how reality is to be construed.

Hegemony is the systematic, institutionalized, and dynamic result of ideological domination and resistance to it. Hegemony is reproduced in specific circumstances as an adaptation to social struggle. Its reproduction depends on repression. As E. P. Thompson puts it:

> Cultural hegemony may define the limits of what is possible, and inhibit the growth of alternative horizons and expectations, there is nothing determined or automatic about this process. Such hegemony can be sustained by the rulers only by the constant exercise of skill, of theater, of concession. Second, such hegemony, even when imposed successfully, does not impose an all embracing view of life; rather, it imposes blinkers, which inhibit vision in certain directions while leaving it clear in others. (Thompson, 1978: 264)

The "blinkers" shape and channel the direction of resistance even as their placement is shaped by the resistant struggle.

This second viewpoint seems more accurate for DTF. Residents resist, but their efforts at opposition continually backfire. An important reason for such failures begins with what it means for them to be there—combined with the definitions of drug abuse and drug treatment.

DRUG ABUSE AS SOCIAL PROBLEM

That drug abuse is a social problem is one of the few assertions that would find majority assent among students of the phenomenon—perhaps a slim majority, but still a majority. A confusing aspect of some social problems is that one is never quite sure what is problematic about them. For instance, is the fact that some people consume heroin the social problem? Or is the social problem the recognition and widely communicated information that some people consume heroin? Or is it that the consumption of heroin is depicted as dangerous to everyone?

A reasonably concise and understandable definition of social problems is given by Charles Reasons (1974: 381), quoting Paul Horton and Gerald Leslie (1970: 4): "A social problem is: (1) a condition (2) affecting a significant number of people in ways considered undesirable (3) about which it is felt that something can be done (4) through collective action." Defined this way, some kinds of social problems do not cause very many conceptual or analytic difficulties. For example, traffic fatalities, or an increase in the number of traffic fatalities, can be such a social problem. The heroin "epidemic" presents difficulties because it is hard to pin down why exactly it is undesirable and in what ways it is undesirable.

As Robert Michaels (1987: 318) points out, "While some Americans are certainly offended by the fact that others consume heroin and derive pleasure from doing so, it is likely that very few would claim that their disgust stems from the sight of consumption per se." Charles Lidz and Andrew Walker (1980) outline what seems to have been perceived as reprehensible about the apparent increase in drug addiction. First, drug usage became associated with a challenge to dominant moral schemas revolving around instrumental-activist values (i.e., values of achievement, mastery of the environment, etc.). In other words, drugs were associated with rebellious youth, radical politics, and hippies. Second, drugs were associated with socially undesirable groups—blacks, Hispanics, and poor people. Third, drugs were associated with crime; that is, it came to be thought that addicts committed crimes to purchase drugs. Finally, a point not stressed by Walker and Lidz is that when drug usage is understood as an "epidemic," there is a fear of infection: with so many more drug addicts running around does the risk not increase that someone I know will "catch" the disease?

In order to understand public policies about drug abuse, it is necessary to understand how it became defined as a problem of use. While the policy of treatment is the primary concern, even the law enforcement emphasis on arresting "dealers" was use-oriented in that the objective is to interdict the connection between supply and demand. All the more so, then, is treatment policy to be understood as use-oriented. The idea is to curtail demand by "curing" people who use drugs. Obviously, policies directed at "prevention" took and continue to take the same approach. Prevention programs hold out the hope of immunizing individuals against using drugs.

Drug Abuse Treatment As Public Policy

The construction of the drug "problem" as a matter of con-sumption explains the basic assumption of drug abuse treat-ment: the primary locus of the problem is the addict. Once drug consumption is identified as the problem, the kinds of things evaluators will look for in determining whether a program 'works' are pre-defined.

As we saw, the social problem of an increase in traffic fatalities, for example, lacks some of the conceptual diffi-culties entailed by the social problem of drug abuse. Imagine that the source of the traffic fatality problem is located in the drivers. Further imagine that other social problems linked to automobiles are similarly located—for example, air pollution, energy shortages, the balance of payments def-icit. In other words, imagine that the ultimate responsibility for these social problems is vested in drivers of automobiles. Now, further imagine that a particular kind of driver, or rather one who drives a particular kind of car, is held up as the paradigm, the model for the automobile "abuser." Let us say that the model driver is one who drives high perform-ance sports cars, preferably red. It is now the job of a policy maker to come up with a program to stop such drivers from driving.

This jocular and perhaps far-fetched example, in reality, is not too different from the scenario faced by policy planners for the treatment of drug addiction in the early 1970s, given the prevalent assumptions. Instead of red sports cars, the model drug was heroin; hence the model drug abuser was a heroin addict. Excluded from consideration were the many people who "abused" prescription drugs, just as in the hypothetical example we exclude those people who, because of some physical impairment, received a physician's prescription allowing them to drive. Also excluded were occasional users, or even more frequent users who did not fit the model of one who is so physically habituated that he or she would experience extremely uncomfortable withdrawal symptoms in the absence of the drug. In other words, the weekend drivers (or users) were excluded.

An implicit image of the model heroin addict dominated treatment program planning. Addicts were involved in crimes, mostly property crimes to "support their habits," but occasionally violent crimes (Inciardi, 1981). They were predominantly members of lower socioeconomic groups. "Minorities" (mainly black and Hispanic) people were over-represented among addicts and were much more often men than women (Richman, 1977).[1]

Based on studies such as that by Alex Richman, Congress passed the Narcotic Addict Treatment Act of 1974 (P.L. 92-281, 88 Stat. 124), which directed federal funds for treatment programs. While initial funding included many experimental programs, by 1979, the year of the Drug Abuse Prevention, Treatment, and Rehabilitation Amendments (P.L. 96-181, 93 Stat. 1309), federally backed drug treatment had shaken down to three approaches or modalities. These modalities were outpatient methadone, outpatient, drug-free counseling, and residential, drug-free programs. There was little support for inpatient, hospital-based detoxification programs, because methadone was used on an outpatient basis for detoxification of heroin addiction.[2] Most residential programs were derived from the therapeutic community model because this was the best-known form of residential treatment.

The Emergence of Therapeutic Communities

Residential therapeutic communities constitute an established and major form of treatment for drug abuse in the United States. Even using a strict definition, there are over five hundred such facilities (DeLeon, 1986). They are small societies in the sense that William Caudill (1958) used that term to describe mental hospitals. One of the explicit intentions in therapeutic communities is to create a micro-culture discrete and distinct from that of the surrounding, larger society.

Therapeutic communities underwent important organizational changes in the middle to late 1970s in reaction to public policies and alterations in their organization. Modeled on the original therapeutic community, Synanon, they proliferated across the country in the 1960s and early 1970s. Usually, they were founded by former members of Synanon. Their purpose was to provide a residential treatment setting for "drug abusers, criminal offenders, and the socially dislocated" (DeLeon, 1985: 825)—in other words, for self-selected members of the underclass. They developed and evolved outside of existing service delivery systems; indeed, they developed self-consciously in opposition to such systems and most other institutions as well. Length of residency was indefinite, but was usually a minimum of one to two years. The staff of the institution were senior residents—that is, those who had been there the longest. When federal policy recognized the therapeutic community as a major treatment modality, drug treatment came under governmental regulation and fiscal support. The two most significant internal changes were a limitation on length of residency and the imposition of non-resident, professional or paraprofessional staff.

One salient feature in the experience of being in a therapeutic community is the pervasive emphasis on the importance of the group. Similar to ideals of the utopian communes in nineteenth-century America, therapeutic communities' central belief is in the efficacy of collective activity to promote change. At the same time, the therapeutic community is a "total institution" not wholly unlike a prison, an army, or a monastery (Goffman, 1961).

The authoritarian and hierarchically organized community with its communitarian ideology interpenetrates with the idea that the social problem of drug abuse is located in the drug users. The assumed nature and location of the drug problem is in turn based on a more general ideology of autonomous individualism. The interpenetration of these two ideologies results in contradiction and conflict within the therapeutic community; at least it does in DTF.

While there is persistent emphasis on the group, day-to-day practices and policies systematically undermine cohesive ties among participants. This contradiction is linked to another, equally important difference. While the target of change in communal movements was society, the target of change in the therapeutic community is the character and lifestyle of its residents. These contradictions are central to the experiences of participants.

The primary social condition that is reproduced inside the therapeutic community is the subordination of the residents to a hierarchical order. With rare exceptions the residents are members of the underclass. Inside the facility as outside of it, their subordination is continually reproduced as the outcome of social conflict. In the larger society, class, race, and gender are the nodal points around which social conflict occurs. Inside the therapeutic community, social conflict is translated into opposition between residents and staff. The general mechanism for achieving this translation is the reconstruction of social identities distinctive for the institution.

Unlike total institutions such as prisons, the therapeutic community does not rely on force or threat of force to maintain social control. The residents' subordination is voluntary, albeit grudgingly so. This unforced subordination depends on beliefs mediated by the manipulation of symbols.

These beliefs are articulated by the creation of distinctive social identities. Social identities related to class, race, and gender are subordinated to, and collapsed into, those of residents (addicts) and staff (rehabilitators).

IDEOLOGIES

In this facility, both the communitarian and individualistic ideologies are *potentially* counter-hegemonic, but *in practice*, their oppositional character is repressed. A radical discourse around which residents could formulate plans of action is unavailable to them. What access they have to a radical discourse is only through the staff, who use it to subordinate the residents.

One radical discourse is the communitarian ideology announced in "The Philosophy." It is radical because it puts identity and meaning up for grabs. It claims that social reality and the persons who make up that reality are in a continuous state of construction, that it is up to the participants in the community to determine who they shall be and what kind of community they shall be part of. But the community in question is not the bounded social establishment of the treatment facility. The community is the group of residents whose lives are managed by the staff persons who are not part of the community, but part of the social establishment that contains the community.

The paradox is so binding on the residents because by seeing through "The Philosophy," which the residents recite every morning, by recognizing its claims for freedom, autonomy, and self-determination as shams, they become fixed in their identities as residents. Their insights about "The Philosophy" are partial. True, it is phoney to affirm autonomy every morning when it is plain to everyone that they live in a restrictive environment. However, what the residents do not recognize is that "The Philosophy" need not be taken as a simple report on the way things are; it can also be taken as a program for the way things could become. This latter insight is unavailable to the residents because the staff repress it.

Parallel to the situation in DTF is a senior citizens' center described by Barbara Myerhoff (1982). In Myerhoff's study, the center is a focus of social life for several hundred elderly, first-generation Jewish immigrants. As a group, these people had become marginalized due to their extreme old age and their ethnicity. According to Myerhoff, they had become disdained and ignored—individuals with "spoiled identities" (Goffman, 1963).

Another parallel is that the people in Myerhoff's study enacted their identities in group performances, just as the residents enact theirs in therapy groups, morning meetings, and a variety of less formal social occasions. However, here the parallel ends, because the people in the senior citizens' center used such opportunities for cultural performances to reconstruct their identities not as spoiled, but as important and valued:

> The consequence is a development of the capacity to lead an examined life. This includes the construction of an explicable, even moral universe despite crushing evidence to the contrary. Center members had achieved this, and their use of rituals and ceremonies to enliven and interpret daily life was remarkable. . . . The old people also felt a certain triumph at having persisted despite the attempts of so many to extinguish them. (Myerhoff, 1982: 107–108)

Whereas the people in Myerhoff's study used rituals and ceremonies to reconstruct valued identities, the residents in DTF find themselves reenacting and thereby confirming their devalued identities despite promises in "The Philosophy" to the contrary.

One of the most striking contrasts is that between Myerhoff's "Life History Class" and many of the therapy groups in DTF. Myerhoff formed a group in which participants were encouraged to recount their life stories. She did so in order to give her informants a forum to express themselves and as a device to facilitate her own data gathering. She reports that the content of the resulting stories fell into four categories: "Being Old," "Life in the Old Country," "Being a Jew," and "Life in America." All of these categories, or kinds of stories, could have been told in such a way as to confirm the devaluation of the story tellers: none of these topics is inherently re-valuing. However, the story tellers in her 'class' took the opportunity to reconstruct experiences that often had been painful, degrading, humiliating, or devaluing so that they became matters of pride. She cites one woman who brought her retarded grandson to the group; Myerhoff comments that for this woman, "He was a kind of badge of honor" (p. 115). Another man brought in a yellow felt star bearing the word "Jude"—a reference to Nazi persecution. Presumably, this too became construed as a "badge of honor."

While the ideology articulated by "The Philosophy" holds out the possibility of similar re-valuing narratives for the residents of the facility, in practice such possibilities are repressed. They are either labeled "war stories" and excluded from conversation altogether, or they are interpreted as signs of personal failure—as badges of shame rather than of honor. For example, one resident had scars on his arms from injections, but these were not injections of drugs; he had donated blood for a fee in order to survive. Rather than viewing him as successful in maintaining himself despite economic hardship, he was viewed as unable to get a good job due to his character flaws and his "poor decision making." Another resident, a woman, had successfully established a bar-brothel, in part as a way to get young prostitutes away from exploitation by pimps. This story, however, was interrupted and characterized as a "war story," and she was not allowed to complete the narrative in a group setting. (Afterwards, she told the story to me privately).

To characterize a narrative as a "war story" represses it completely. "War stories," in the ideology of the facility, are tales that recount successes in the "dope fiend" way of life, and as such they are not proper fare for conversation. They are interrupted, and if the teller persists, s/he is punished. There is no opportunity for reinterpretation or re-valuing. Other stories that might be interpreted as stories of survivorship instead become stories of failure, personal shortcomings, or "poor decision making." In such cases, aspects of the story that might redeem the self-esteem of the resident are excluded by the way they are interpreted. These repressions interdict references to narratives that could imply anything positive other than the lifestyle approved in the ideology of the facility.

While personal identity narratives are manipulated by means of repression, so are group identities manipulated, but the latter repression operates in a somewhat different fashion. Social identities based on race, gender, or class are excluded by characterizing them as irrelevant or unimportant. Here, repression does not affect personal memories of individuals; it affects present perception of social realities.

There is another contrast with the senior citizens' center described by Myerhoff. While the center participants were all elderly, Jewish, and poor, there were as many grounds for differences among them as for similarities. Thus, although all were elderly, they were not in the same age cohort; and while all had been immigrants, they had not entered the United States at the same time. While all were Jewish, they varied in the ways they had related to that religious tradition. Some had grown up in major cities, while others had been reared in rather rural *shtetls*. Their reconstruction of a common cultural background of *Yiddishkeit* drew on other cultural sources to which each of them had a different and variable relationship—"Old World, Yiddish, Jewish, modern, American, Californian, secular, and sacred" (Myerhoff, 1986: 264). The cultural unity that they constructed integrated these differences; it did not submerge them. The achieved unity depended as much on diversity as on commonality.

In contrast, residents in DTF are given a unity in a way that requires the submergence of variation. In part, this strategy of achieving unity through the obliteration of differences comes from the tradition of Alcoholics Anonymous. In A.A., each member is just an alcoholic, regardless of station in life, age, race, or gender. But variation in A.A. can be seen *between* A.A. groups. In this facility, all residents are thrown together, so there is no choice in selecting a group based on compatibility of social identities. Instead, such variation is repressed by denying its significance: there is a pretense of homogeneity, which is enforced through rules and routines. The enforcement of repression is articulated in the rhetoric of the communitarian ideal in which everyone is 'essentially' the same.

The communitarian ideology is a fundamental part of therapeutic communities; it comes from Synanon and the philosophy developed by Charles Dederich. Dederich's self-perceived mission was to erect a community that offered an alternative to mainstream American society. This project was very much in the tradition of utopian communities throughout America's history. What set Dederich's project apart was that the initial members of Synanon were drug addicts, so that part of Synanon's communitarian ideology was directed against its members as well as against the larger society.

Synanon assumed that its members were immature, that they needed to grow up again, and that Synanon would provide a corrective environment for this regrowth. At the same time there was an assumption that they had an intrinsic character flaw that could never be corrected. This is why Synanon operated under the assumption of a permanent commitment to the community. As long as Synanon operated as a utopian commune, this character flaw theory was not a significant issue in day-to-day interactions, because the Synanon environment was supposed to provide an antidote to its members' character disorders. However, when the Synanon model was applied to therapeutic communities where the goal was rehabilitation rather than permanent commitment, this part of the communitarian ideology underwent some changes. The therapeutic community not only had to provide an antidote but had to have a prophylactic effect so that the addict would not return to addiction and could return to society. The goal for therapeutic communities was not merely remission of the character disorder; it had to become one of cure. The issue was no longer just a matter of maintaining a better (ideal?) society in the community; it also became one of producing a better person. Once this issue was raised, the discourse of the autonomous individual became an important part of the ideological framework of therapeutic communities.

The ideology of the autonomous individual is the other potentially radical tradition that is dispensed by the staff to the residents. This ideology is enunciated in two written texts: "The Awareness System" and the book *Help Yourself to Happiness*. Autonomous individuality can be radically emancipatory. Indeed, its history in Western culture is one of freeing people from the restrictions of corporate identities grounded in kinship, estate, and other pre-modern social arrangements. In sum, universalistic individualism liberates people from the oppressions of particularistic communitarianism.

In DTF the ideology of individualism is manifest in the formulation or, more accurately, the reproduction of the addict-resident identity and the denial of alternative identities for residents, especially those of race, class, and gender. In addition, the addict-resident identity is reproduced in opposition to the staff-counselor identity. The reproduction of identities depends on repression.

Acts of repression are clearly observable and easily identifiable at the level of concrete interactions. The staff enforce rules that prohibit residents from reciprocal exchange of goods and services. Nascent subgroups among residents are labeled "cliques" and broken up by isolating the members from one another. Associations among residents based on racial identification are called racist and similarly discouraged and interdicted. Gender is officially repudiated as a basis for differentiating among residents; at the same time, sexual liaisons between men and women are strictly forbidden, thus reinforcing gender asymmetries. The economy of the facility exploits residents' labor and enforces material dependency, identifies that dependency as characteristic emotional dependency, and conceals the mutual fiscal dependence between residents and the treatment program.

These acts of repression are coordinated with the exclusion, in group settings, of narratives that would re-value residents' identities. The only permissible narratives that would explain the residents' present circumstances are those that are grounded in the identity of the criminal addict, or the "dope fiend" way of life. Such narratives are framed by a theory that locates both cause and blame within the resident. According to this theory, the reasons that led people to become members of the subordinated group of residents all stem from the fact that, in the words of "The Awareness System," "A dependent person lives an ineffective life because a dependent person is not responsible for his own life." Present delicts are explained the same way. When residents break rules or fail to progress in the program, the character flaw of dependency is pointed out as the only permissible explanation. The result of such explanations is to reproduce the addict-resident identity.

IDENTITIES

Punishment is by no means tangential to the central object of treatment in DTF. Knapp (1989) uses the institution of punishment to explore the concept of identity, personhood, the past, and memory. He notes that punishment is "a social practice that, perhaps more obviously than any other, assumes that past events have an intrinsic relevance to present action." (p. 134). He goes on to argue,

> on this view we don't punish people because we believe that they are in some mysterious sense metaphysically identical to the self that existed in the moment the bad act occurred. . . . Instead, we punish them in order to make them identify with the act in a way that will *constitute* their taking responsibility for it. . . . We want to cause people, in other words, to anticipate that they will be unable to *deny* their identity with the selves they are when they commit whatever crime they contemplate committing. (Knapp, 1989: 138)

The institution of punishment insures, and even causes, identification of selves through time. It is an institutionalized way of maintaining or establishing continuity of identity. If this be the basis for the impulse to punishment, different *forms* of punishment would reveal different conceptions of identity.

Almost all the punitive measures in DTF are of the restrictive variety; they take away freedoms. Moreover, they take away not just any kind of freedom, but that of communication.

What is known in the facility as a "full restriction" applies to communicative interactions. Residents who are "on restriction" are not allowed to have visits, passes, or telephone calls. When they leave the facility on a necessary errand (e.g., court appearances, medical appointments) they are required to have "strength"—another resident who accompanies them and whose main function is to insure that the person "on restriction" has no unauthorized contacts. Of course the paradigm case of the communicative restriction is the liberal use of "communication bans." The communicative restriction as the main form of punishment can be contrasted with punishments that were formerly used but that have been curtailed. The older form of punishment relied much more heavily on public ridicule or shaming. Residents were required to dress in ridiculous costumes (wear diapers, dunce caps, etc.) or carry demeaning signs. Displays of shame have been eliminated, for the most part, and almost exclusive emphasis is now placed on the therapeutic and corrective benefits of confession. Of course, confession is a monologue, not a dialogue, and not truly communicative. The pillory has been replaced by the confessional.[3]

Confession relieves guilt as an inner truth is brought forth. The process of revealing an inner truth can be likened to the Michelangeline notion of "liberating" the form of a sculpture held in a block of marble. To carry the analogy further, the residents present a refractory medium as does the marble, and the process of liberation is one of chipping away the obscuring crust to liberate a purified essence of personhood.

The objective of treatment in DTF is to make new identities, and punishment is the principal method. The kind of punishment used is subtractive; it strips away that which conceals inner truth, identity, and essence. The concept of identity predicates the existence of an inner core self, which must be purified.

This analysis should not be taken to imply that the shift in punishment style has come about from some profound philosophical speculations. Much of the shaming was eliminated in response to economic necessity and the demands of DTF's funding source and collaboration with the correctional system. Too much of the shaming drove away residents, so that neither containment nor surveillance could be achieved. The change in punishment technique manifested the conceptual change.

Repression and public confession might seem contradictory, but the way they are practiced in DTF shows how they can work together. In addition, those practices show how a communal conception of social life can be coordinated with an individualistic conception of person. The point of contact is sameness of essence. To quote from "The Philosophy": "Until we confront ourselves in the eyes and hearts of others . . . we will be alone, where else but in this common ground can we find such a mirror." The group, here, provides a mirror, a uniform reflection of the self. Implicit in this view is an inner sameness to all people; that is what forms the mirror. Being part of the group is a matter of recognizing this inner sameness, and all the procedures followed at DTF can be understood as attempts to let this inner sameness shine forth. Therefore, public confession strips away confining variation, allowing individuals to join with the group in a merger of like identities.

Inner sameness is also the point of contact with the conception of the autonomous individual. Autonomous individuals compete in the marketplace, but in order to have a free market, there must be equality among negotiators. If the philosophical basis for equality is a Rousseau-like human nature, then this natural essence must be the same for us all. Strip away the trappings of civilization, the differences of station and rank that it imposes among people, and what you have left is an identical, core, moral basis for equality.

This essentialist conception of person also helps explain how a regime of surveillance, control, and punishment can be rationalized as drug treatment. By taking drugs, addicts subvert and contaminate their natural human essence. This is a moral crime, one that must be prevented in the future and one for which they must atone by cleansing confessions. The cleansing process requires that superficial variation must be put aside or chipped away to get down to the root of the problem, one that all addicts have in common—their addict personalities.

The stated goal of DTF's program description to its funding source is to "modify the resident's attitudes and values," not just about drugs but about their ways of life and personal identities. This kind of goal seems to be pretty clear-cut ideological domination, but where my analysis differs from DTF's program statement is at the word 'modify.' I argue that the ideological domination or hegemony as practiced in DTF does not modify or change, but in fact *confirms* the social identities of the residents as devalued and powerless. It even confirms their passive positions as consumers in the illicit drug market. A peculiar bit of evidence supports this conclusion.

According to nationally based statistical surveys of drug treatment effectiveness, the "success rate" of treatment programs like DTF (as well as the other major drug treatment modalities) has a range of about 15 percent to 20 percent (see Biernacki, 1986 for an analysis of the analysis). These statistical data are resemble the impressionistic estimate made by the director of DTF about its "success rate"— about 15 percent. These numbers suggest that DTF has a high success rate (85 percent) in reproducing drug addicts.

A reasonable question at this point would be why places like DTF are needed to reproduce addicts? In this facility, residents are continually 'reminded' that they are drug addicts, criminals, whores, liars, and so on. Indeed, much of the "therapy" seems to consist of such reminders of "spoiled identities" (Goffman, 1963), along with directives that they ought not to enact these identities. The residents should be drug addicts who do not take drugs, criminals who do not commit crimes. What is the point of these 'reminders'? Is it possible that without reminding, the residents would forget who they are? In a fascinating way, I think the answer to this question is 'yes.'

Patterns of institutional practices reproduce identities of persons who participate in them. In DTF, there is one central identity that is reproduced, that of the addict-resident. A thematic, indeed definitive, set of practices contributes to this reproduction: the heavy reliance on a confessional style of interaction. This can be seen in the way therapy groups are conducted, certainly in the way "crisis groups" operate, and it can be seen with slight modification in such ritualized practices as "in-depths." A confessional style *can be* creative and liberating, as the example from Barbara Myerhoff's study reveals. In that case, participants took the opportunity of what could be called public confession to construct re-valuing narratives of and for themselves. An essential ingredient in that situation was that the 'confessions' of the participants were largely open to their own interpretations of what was relevant and how narrative elements should be evaluated. The relative lack of staff control on symbolizing evident in Myerhoff's study presents a marked contrast to the 'confessions' of residents in DTF.

Confessions in DTF are rigidly constrained in their content. What residents talk about is prescribed and limited by repressions. A 'good, relevant' confession for a resident definitely does not consist in a recounting of experiences of, say, being black in urban America. It does consist of tales of 'wrongdoing'—incidents of drug use in the facility, sexual interactions, unauthorized phone calls, and the like. "Openness and honesty" consist of appropriate confessions, which are part of personal identity narratives, which, in turn, build up the addict-resident identity. That is how DTF reproduces addicts. Recursive pressures at the institutional level shape these confessional practices, and residents themselves participate in them to make gains in the moral economy of the facility so that they can demonstrate "progress in treatment" to concerned outsiders (probation officers, judges, etc.).

As residents pass through DTF, they are supposed to be transformed, but what they do is temporarily adjust to the demands of the situation. The form of this adjustment contributes to the reproduction of their original identities. It is in this sense that the residents' participation in their own oppression can be characterized as voluntary. To them, DTF is just another in a long line of institutional sites in which their identities are reproduced. These sites would include their families, the neighborhoods in which they grew up, jail, school, and even such sites as "dope houses" and "copping areas." The irony is that the very practices that are supposed to change the residents from addicts into something else insure their continued existence as addicts as effectively as does a "dope house."

Solidarity and Censoriousness

The continual reproduction of the addict-resident identity brings back the question of the lack of collective resistance. If the residents are continually identified as having common characteristics, why do they not assert their own interests against what they themselves recognize as oppressive conditions? A study by Thomas Mathiesen (1965) of a Norwegian correctional facility may shed some light on the problem. In his study Mathiesen was struck by the lack of collective resistance on the part of the inmates and their overall lack of peer solidarity.

Mathiesen's facility has no exact counterpart in the United States. It is a combination jail and psychiatric treatment facility. The main difference between the Norwegian facility and the drug treatment facility is that in the former the inmates are restrained by physical force; hence control is not entirely dependent on ideology. In other respects, however, there are interesting parallels. In both cases the inmates are congregated and at the same time subjected to individualized treatment. Both inmate groups hold a devalued identity according to standards in the society at large, and both groups are dominated by a staff within the facility.

In comparison with inmates in a conventional Norwegian prison and with workers in a factory, Mathiesen found a relatively low degree of peer solidarity. He also found that the inmates engaged in a relatively high degree of competition and what he calls "censoriousness" directed against one another. Censoriousness takes the form of accusations of not living up to standards of justice and fairness. Mathiesen offers three hypotheses about his observations. He says that, "under otherwise equal conditions, the probability of finding censoriousness of competing individuals rather than peer solidarity as a reaction to perceived illegitimate power":

1. Increases as the inmates perceive themselves to be in a poor bargaining position vis-à-vis the staff.

2. Increases as the sense of honor in association with others among one's peers decreases below a certain 'minimum.'

3. Increases as lack of subcultural tradition outside [the facility] increases. (Mathiesen, 1965: 221–223)

Findings in the present study tend to confirm Mathiesen's hypotheses, but the differences between the two establishments yield different explanations for this 'fit.'

His first hypothesis about the bargaining position relates to the material or economic contribution of the inmates to the establishment. We have seen that the residents in the drug treatment facility are an important part of its economy. However, their contributions are disguised and concealed through acts of repression. Therefore, their *perceived* bargaining position is much weaker than their actual contributions would support. While the residents are able to see through the ideological claim that their work is "therapeutic," they remain unaware of how it supports the total economy of the establishment. Perhaps even more importantly, the residents do not understand their role in the purchase-of-service contract with the funding source for the facility. They do not see themselves as "paying customers," yet their position is not much different from that of anyone who relies on third-party payments for services. The success of repressions leads the residents to misrecognize their bargaining potential; hence their efforts at resistance are misdirected.

In regard to the second hypothesis, the residents certainly do have a low sense of honor, but perhaps it is not

much lower than it was among the participants in Myerhoff's study before they re-valued themselves. In the facility the low sense of honor is directly connected to the reproduction of the identity of addict-resident. This reproductive
process derives to some extent from the situation at DTF
and to some extent from the already existing identity of the
addict-resident. This reproductive process is not creative or
reaffirming; it depends on repressions. Time and again residents make a gesture that could lead to a re-valuing performance, and just as repeatedly the path to a re-valuation is
interdicted by repression. Therefore, the low sense of honor
should not be seen as a given, a matter of circumstance; it
requires the active application of repressive force.

Mathiesen's third hypothesis pertains to a lack of subcultural tradition. The question of whether the residents in
this facility are members of one or several subcultures could
lead into a tortuous controversy. For instance, Michael Agar
(1973) argues in favor of a subculture of heroin addicts, and
so to some extent do Edward Preble and John Casey (1969).
However, the residents are not just heroin addicts, and it is
certainly questionable whether their presupposed drug dependency could be related to any kind of common values or
norms. However, the residents are members of groups
around which identity-asserting discourses have been formulated. Such discourses might include those of black power,
feminism, and some more or less Marxist discourses relating
to class. The question of whether these discourses or other
affirmations of group identity would lead to true subcultures or reflect existing ones is outside the scope of this
study. However, what is relevant and ascertainable is that,
within the facility, extra-situational grounding of group
identities is regularly repressed.

Social cohesion among residents is perhaps the primary
focus of repressive acts. The creation or reproduction of the
addict-resident identity discourages solidarity among residents because it is coupled with social atomization. At-

tempts by the residents to establish integrative social bonds are always interrupted and sometimes punished. Therefore, subcultural affiliation is ideologically irrelevant in the facility because it is made to be so through repressive acts.

The main difference between Mathiesen's study and this one is that Mathiesen's source is the social structure. In the present study, the applicability of his hypotheses stems from a pattern of repression. A good part of the difference between Mathiesen's interpretations and those presented here has to do with the importance of physical force. The more that oppression relies on force and less on ideology, the more direct is the relationship between social structure and acts of repression: there is less reliance on symbolic mediation.

Another difference is that Mathiesen's hypotheses refer to "perceived illegitimate power." This Weberian notion that power is or can be legitimated is not supported by my findings. Legitimacy seems to have little to do with the residents' acquiescence to control and domination. They know they are controlled and oppose it with the only means they believe they have at their disposal—individual acts of resistance.

AUTHORITY, POWER, AND REALITY

Rather than a matter of legitimacy, a more incisive distinction is that between power and authority. Authority, unlike power, is an ideological phenomenon. The ability to influence others based on authority rests on claims of 'rightness' both in a moral sense and in the sense of correctness and accuracy. In this facility power masquerades as authority. Because authority depends partly on being correct, on more accurately representing a particular state of affairs, ultimately on a superior understanding of the nature of the world, in social conflicts in DTF the character of reality is at stake. Here, social control is not accomplished by means of lock and key, but rather by occlusion, disguise, misdirection—in sum, by repression.

Much of the success of repression depends on claims of rationality. Such claims of rationality, perhaps not surprisingly, are linked to the ideology of the autonomous individual. Therefore, it is by no means accidental that an important part of the routine in the facility is a 'class' that studies the book *Help Yourself to Happiness*. The thesis of the book is that you (the reader) can be happy if only you make rational decisions and carry them out. The theme of the 'class' is that the residents have gotten themselves into the mess they are in now (i.e., residents in a drug treatment facility) because they have made irrational decisions. In order to become happy and avoid future messes, they must learn how to be rational. A corollary to this theme is that the residents have misunderstood the nature of reality and have to be taught how to understand it properly. The underlying assumption and message is that there is *a reality* accessible to rational understanding. While this theme is developed in depth in the 'class,' it is also reiterated in every explicit interpretation of residents' behavior.

The appeal to rationality lies at the foundation of the ideological framework of the treatment program. However, its ideological character remains hidden. This is because "one of the most important general functions of ideology is the way in which it turns uncertain and fragile cultural resolutions and outcomes into a pervasive naturalism" (Willis, 1981: 162). Willis goes on to show how this affects the British working-class boys in his study:

> The least challenged and most mystified cultural productions from below are shaped, concretized and supported to form a real and lived common denominator which allows all classes to come together into a kind of consensus which is the reproduction of the status quo and the stage-army show of democracy. . . . For the working class it often marks the break from one absolutism, bourgeois ideology, to a profounder one: *the*

law of nature, the rule of common sense [emphasis added].
. . . For "the lads" this hegemony of commonsense surrounds
them all the time. (Willis, 1981: 162)

The "lads" see through the false claims of middle-class
cultural standards, but they cannot see through what seems
to be the natural way of the world: "The way of the world
is the way of work" (Willis, 1981: 162). In the same way,
the residents may see through the ideological claims in "The
Philosophy," and some of the more perspicacious may even
see through the claims about "effective living" that are
made in "The Awareness System." However, claims that
rely on common sense, the common perceptions of everyday, concrete realities, and the common denominators of life
experiences seem as inaccessible to penetration as the "ax-
iom" that the way of the world is the way of work.

Some of the most important of these commonsense realities are social realities both inside the facility and outside it.
An implicit assumption in *Help Yourself to Happiness* (one
that is suggested by the very title of the book) is that success
and therefore happiness (the two are equated) will naturally
follow if only one diligently applies reason along with persistent effort. In its extreme form this is the Horatio Alger
story, which ignores systematic and structural inequality in
American society. But even in its less extreme form, as it is
articulated in the facility, the basic message is the same.

The less extreme form of the Horatio Alger story does
not completely ignore such social realities as institutionalized racism, gender inequality, and the systematic limitations of opportunities for people from lower-class backgrounds. The less extreme form of this story acknowledges
that a resident is unlikely to become president of General
Motors. Instead, it says that individuals can overcome lia-
bilities, break through social barriers, and come to enjoy the
middle-class American dream. The story, as it is told in the
facility, points to opportunities that would seem to validate
it. For instance, residents can overcome educational deficits

by acquiring a high-school equivalency degree, and then they can go on to a vocational college or even a four-year institution of higher learning to obtain marketable job skills. If they have a criminal record (most residents do) they can aspire, one day, to have it erased through a governor's pardon; one of the counselors did this. The message is that both incurred and inherent social disabilities can be ameliorated, if not entirely eliminated, through judicious use of opportunities for self-improvement. Individuals can surmount obstacles even though they may be members of marginalized social groups. The goal for each resident is to become a productive, law-abiding, middle-class citizen (in the peculiarly elastic American sense).

There are some important implications of this modified Horatio Alger narrative. First, it undermines solidarity among residents based on their common subordinate status by promising that *individuals* can escape from subordination. Second, it denies the material significance of membership in marginalized and/or oppressed social groups and thus excludes radical discourses such as feminism, black power, and so on. Finally, by affirming the possibility of individual success, it links reality claims (i.e., claims that its "world report" is accurate and correct) with moral claims: not only is it possible to achieve middle-class success but it is morally good to aspire to it.

One of the most important effects of the ideology of individualism is that it modifies the radical potential of the communitarian ideology. Whereas the communitarian ideology derived from Synanon implied a fundamental critique of American culture and society, in DTF this radical critique is shifted away from 'society' and onto the residents as individuals. The tradition of utopian communes in America, however much the communes may have controlled the lives of their members, always located the basic problems of life in the social arrangements of the larger society. In the facility, certain criticism of particular injustices may be allowed (e.g., racism is acknowledged), but these are denied as the cause of residents' infelicitous situation. Instead, the cause is attributed to the residents themselves. The meaning of "The Philosophy" is not that the residents "will become as we could be" because the community offers a radically different, growth-promoting social environment; it is rather because it demands that residents reform their individual values, perceptions, and lifestyles.

Social realities inside the facility appear to negate social inequalities outside of it. For example, gender and racial equality are publicly affirmed in both word and deed in the system of the program. This is the egalitarianism of the community.

Women and men, black and white, gain privileges, are punished and assigned jobs, and generally progress through the program without regard to race and gender. On the other hand, women's sexuality is treated as if it needs external controls, while men have to control themselves. Female residents in positions of authority are taught to 'relate' to their subordinates, while men are taught to command them. The physical space in the facility is male space, while space for women is specially marked. Women are taught to be 'good mothers' as part of their rehabilitation from drug addiction, while men are not required to become 'good fathers.'

Similarly, helping networks for black residents are treated with suspicion at best, and DTF attempts to extract the residents from them. Black identity is indiscriminately associated with the "dope fiend" way of life. The very negation of racial inequality inside the facility short-circuits questions like how it comes to be that black people are grossly over-represented compared to the overall population of the city.

The moral economy promoted by the ideology of the treatment program obscures the material economy by which the facility runs. Residents, staff, and even functionaries in the funding system fail to recognize the mutual dependency of the residents and the program. They all regard the program as a government enterprise of which the residents are the beneficiaries (or victims, as the case may be). As consumers of services, the residents are excluded from decisions about the structure and form of resource distribution, and the process of distribution remains concealed as part of the accepted infrastructure—sort of like sewerage and water mains.

The communitarian ideology establishes an egalitarian collectivity whose sole interests are those of the community of residents. Competing group identities are negated by means of repression. The individualistic ideology atomizes the residents, separates each and all from their fellows as particular 'cases' with unique needs and careers, and negates interests that the residents may have as a collectivity. The net result, one that is not entirely unintended, is to reproduce the social position of the addict-resident. A particular effect of this reproduction is to reproduce the position in which the residents have no say in the conditions of consumption of drugs.

While a number of authors (e.g., Lidz and Walker, 1980; Rosenbaum, 1981; Weppner, 1983) have commented on the fact that treatment programs seem to be just another part of the life-world of addiction, they have not specified how the routines in such programs result in this fit. Social identities related to race, class, and gender are reproduced by excluding their significance from public recognition in the facility. Clearly, public talk of drugs could not be subjected to such wholesale exclusions since the express purpose of the facility is drug treatment. However, drug talk is selective in interesting and revealing ways.

Omissions in talk about drugs suggest that an important part of the message of the treatment program is that the residents have no material interests in the conditions of drug consumption. In contrast to this message, consider the relatively recent history of marijuana use. In the late 1960s, after having been confined to certain limited sectors of the population, marijuana entered the general youth market. In fact, marijuana use became an important part of what was for a while a youth counterculture. At the time, mere use or possession of the drug was a serious felony in most jurisdictions in the United States. Also, most of the marijuana on the market was imported. Marijuana users recognized their collective interests in the conditions of consumption of the commodity. The legalization of marijuana became a quasi-political movement. While this movement may have had little success, its rather informal organization did have important and observable effects on the marijuana market. Today, many jurisdictions have effectively decriminalized possession and use. A great proportion of marijuana on the market is produced domestically. Moreover, the 'quality' or drug content of the commodity is significantly higher than it was in the late 1960s.

The particular outcomes of the marijuana story are less significant for present purposes than the process of what occurred. In the case of marijuana, a group of users gave public articulation to their collective, material interests with significant results. An analogous process among the addict-residents is interdicted by repressions and exclusions. The result is to reproduce atomized individuals without recognition of any, similar collective interests, to reinforce their relatively powerless position vis-à-vis the commodities they consume, and to insure the status quo of the political economy of the drug world.

A number of studies (e.g., Biernacki, 1986) have demonstrated that a 'cure' for drug addiction is largely a matter of idiosyncratic and circumstantial factors. Moreover, this perspective is acknowledged as correct by drug treatment policy functionaries such as those in the funding source for this facility. The implication is that, however effective a particular treatment program may be, the program itself cannot produce 'cures.' It is appropriate to ask what it does produce.

'NEW' SOCIAL IDENTITIES

The claim by this facility and by therapeutic communities in general is that their programs produce a change in the characters of the residents. However, there is no evidence in support of this claim in the present ethnographic study, or in any other study that has addressed this issue. While such a claim regarding character or personality is questionable on its face, a claim that such a program might affect the social identities of participants is at least plausible. In fact, the program seems to be extremely effective in reproducing the social identities of the residents, especially in regard to their relative powerlessness and subordinate status.

There is a certain irony in the fact that analysts concerned with drug treatment policy have stressed the need to generalize residents' behavior in therapeutic communities to the situations they confront after discharge; for example, J. David Hawkins and Norman Wacker (1983 and 1986) make this explicit. What most residents 'learn' in the facility is what they knew implicitly all along: their economic, political, and social dependency is well nigh unbreachable. Those aspects of the program that offer some real possibility of changing their social circumstances are relatively minimal. High-school equivalency classes, referrals to vocational rehabilitation programs, referrals to low-income housing programs, and so on are adjunct and auxiliary parts of rehabilitation within the facility. They are treated as peripheral to the 'real stuff' of therapy, which is aimed at the moral reform of character.

In everyday, mundane ways this 'real stuff' of therapy takes the form of a continuous struggle between residents and counselors. The struggle comes about because the staff are the most immediate agents of repression against the residents, and they are brought to act as repressive agents due to extra-situational forces and constraints. It is the staff who must answer to the administrative hierarchy of the social service agency of which this facility is a part, and to the funding source and the state correctional system.

While the staff members refer to themselves as therapists, the goals of the treatment program are regulatory. There are three primary duties of the staff with respect to program goals. First, the staff are supposed to keep the residents in the program for at least thirty days; that is, the staff must contain the residents and keep them under surveillance. Second, they should make sure that the residents do not consume illicit drugs. Finally, they should try to reduce the possibility that residents might get arrested by demanding a strict account of residents' activities when they leave the facility.

The staff have at their disposal mainly ideological means to meet these regulatory goals. They must somehow persuade the residents to stay in the program. While the staff use some direct interventions to curtail drug use such as searches and urine tests, the most important instrument is persuasion. In general, the staff must find a way to convince the residents that it is in their best interests to stay in the program, to refrain from drug use, and to avoid acting in ways that risk arrest. The idea that these goals are in the best interest of the residents allows the staff to characterize their own actions as therapeutic. It is also what makes the instrument of control so clearly ideological.

The dilemma for counselors is that they have to reconcile competing and often contradictory discourses about reality and what should be done about it. As functionaries in an establishment charged with regulation and surveillance of criminal law breakers and social deviants, they must intervene to demonstrate their mastery of the residents to monitors from the criminal justice system—most often probation officers and bail monitors. As therapists, they should encourage the greatest possible degree of autonomy in residents. As counselors in a therapeutic community, they must insist that residents adhere to the rules of the program and must dispense the belief that the community itself is the decisive agent in the residents' rehabilitation. Finally, as persons, they must modulate their own beliefs and attitudes about the residents' lifestyles in general and drug use in particular to harmonize with these other principal discourses. The position of counselor, then, is one of considerable strain and conflict.

Not the least of the conflicts surrounds the issue of putative manipulativeness on the part of residents. It has become a virtual truism among practitioners in drug treatment that a significant aspect of addicts' character disorder is a proclivity to manipulate others in order to gain advantage and gratification. The counselors in this facility are acutely aware of this generalization, and they believe they must constantly guard against being manipulated by the residents.

If the counselors "give in" to manipulations, they encourage the character disorder, thereby defeating therapeutic goals. Perhaps even more to the point is the danger that by being manipulated the counselors will enter into complicity with residents' corrupt and corrupting desires. Thus, there is an inescapable moral component: addiction and the "dope fiend" way of life are not bad merely because they are harmful but because they are evil. The counselors must always be on guard against contamination by this evil. Their very association, their proximity to the residents, raises the suspicion of possible contamination. Therefore, the counselors must maintain a certain social distance. The maintenance of distance becomes another source of strain and conflict for counselors because they cannot be so distant that they cannot perform the other tasks involved in their jobs.

As stated in "The Awareness System," "The dependent person engages in either passive or aggressive behavior because he has found these effective for him in manipulating other people's behavior." The implication is that manipulative behavior is deceptive behavior; the aggression of a dependent person is bluster, the passivity of a dependent person seduction. If the residents were not dependent people, they would not have to rely on false fronts. Their aggressive behavior would be backed up by real power, so they could command rather than bluster. Alternatively, their passive behavior would be founded on security, so they could request rather than seduce. Perhaps the most interesting aspect of this discourse on dependency and manipulation is that both are attributed to the character of the addict-resident.

Dependency is an intrinsic part of their persons and is manifested in their manipulativeness.

Attributing dependency to the residents calls for the counselors to discourage dependency by not giving into attempts at manipulation. However, the residents really are dependent on the counselors. They must get permission to leave the facility, they need permission to go to their bedrooms, and they rely on counselors to provide positive reports to probation officers and the court. To encourage autonomy among residents would be to change the relationship between residents and counselors dramatically: the counselors would have to give up much of their power over the residents, something they cannot do if they are to meet the requirements of surveillance and regulation.

Including dependency as an integral part of the identity of the residents resolves conflicts for the counselors. The real relationship with residents can be disregarded so that counselors do not have to abrogate their position of power; this dependency, since it is a character flaw, can be cured, thereby allowing the counselors to act like therapists. Furthermore, labeling the residents as dependent justifies not giving in to residents' attempts to "manipulate" them and thus permits counselors to maintain a comfortable social distance.

From the residents' point of view, this dependency discourse is an important part of what they have to learn to be successful in the facility; it outlines the rules of the game they have to play. They have to relieve the counselors of strain and conflict by pretending to be autonomous when they are not. They have to acquiesce to counselors' controlling their lives because the counselors have authority, not because they have power. Therefore, it is in the interest of the residents to uphold the masquerade of power as authority, and to do this they enter into a silent collusion with the counselors.

When anyone advises or persuades another person to do something "for their own good," one is entitled to be suspicious of their motives and/or look for evidence of ideological domination and false consciousness. Alvin Gouldner (1976) makes a pertinent distinction: propaganda is a kind of discourse designed to mislead by its promulgators (i.e., propagandizers do not themselves believe it), whereas ideological discourse is to be believed by everyone. The persuasions of the staff are ideological; they themselves believe what they tell the residents. These ideological persuasions create a false consciousness in that they disguise the fact that they are the principal means of controlling the residents.

The problem in attributing a false consciousness to a group, especially a subordinated group, is that such an attribution implies that someone else knows the 'real' interests of the group better than do the members. On the one hand the program goals *are* in the best interest of the residents; on the other hand the control that depends on such a discourse is not in their best interest *and the residents know that.* What they do not know is how to objectify this "best interest" discourse as a means of domination. This is why it is a matter of false consciousness for the residents; they know their best interest is not served, but they cannot articulate how it would be served. It is also a matter of false consciousness for the staff, who see themselves as therapists and helpers, not dominators. In fact, the counseling staff believe that they are helping to liberate the residents from drug addiction and other self-destructive behavior.

The residents, for their part, have to believe the same thing. But they have to believe it for different reasons. Whereas the counselors need the belief in order to reconcile conflicting discourses and alleviate role strain, the residents have to believe it because alternative beliefs are systematically excluded from symbolic representation. Each group has an investment in the ideology of the facility, although neither group is entirely comfortable with it. That is why less than 10 percent of the residents complete the program, and among the counseling staff only the director has remained at the facility for much more than two years. The 'willing suspension of disbelief' can be sustained for only so long. In his overview of the "helping professions" Murray Edelman (1974: 298–299) puts it this way:

> It is of course the ambiguity in the relationship, and the ambivalence in the professional and the client, that gives the linguistic usage its flexibility and potency. . . . Many clients want help, virtually all professionals think they are providing it, and sometimes they do so. . . . The political relationship seems nonexistent until it is selfconsciously questioned. . . . We normally fail to recognize this catalytic capacity of language because we think of linguistic terms and syntactic structures as signals rather than as symbols. . . . But if a word is a symbol that condenses and rearranges feelings, memories, perceptions, beliefs, and expectations, then it evokes a particular structuring of beliefs and emotions, a structuring that varies with people's social situations. . . . Language as symbol catalyzes a subjective world in which uncertainties are clarified and appropriate courses of action become clear. . . . In the symbolic worlds evoked by the language of the helping professions speculations and verified facts readily merge with each other. Language dispels the uncertainty in speculation, changes facts to make them serve status distinctions, and reinforces ideology.

The residents of this facility 'put up with' their situation because the ideology of the program is the only one they have. They cannot formulate an alternative ideology because their attempts to do so are repressed. Repressive acts interdict the articulation of discourses for radical change. At the same time, they interdict those social actions that could lead to collective resistance. In the absence of collective resistance, the only option is individual resistance, which ultimately contributes to the residents' subordination. Radical social change through collective action requires an alternative to the existing order. When alternatives are repressed, hegemonic domination is strengthened. Hegemony cannot persist without repression, and repression is perhaps the principal mechanism of its survival and reproduction.

NOTES

Chapter 2

1. This is a very rough estimate made by the director of the program. The main reason that the estimate is so approximate is that the same person may be referred by several sources. However, if the prospective client is on probation or parole, the referral is attributed to the probation/parole agent.

2. The bail monitoring program acts as a consultant to the court for setting bail. It screens all arrestees and makes recommendations to the courts regarding bail. Persons who say they want drug treatment are often referred to DTF as a condition of bail. Their participation in the treatment program is then monitored by a functionary of the agency who reports to the court.

3. Usually this is the MMPI (Minnesota Multiphasic Personality Inventory), which can be administered by anyone, since it is a paper and pencil instrument. The results are interpreted by the consulting psychologist.

4. These include the completion of the physical examination, completion of a written autobiography, completion of a written treatment plan, possibly a psychological evaluation, and possibly a final disposition of the resident's legal status depending on how relevant this is thought to be by the counseling staff.

5. Normally visits are allowed only on the weekends. Any visit must be requested in writing by noon of the preceding Wednesday. A description of residents' relationship to visitors and the reason for the visit are required. If the visitor and the reason are satisfactory, the visit still may not be approved if the resident is not making sufficient "progress in treatment." In this case, the visit was unusual because visits are rarely allowed within the first thirty days.

6. She had been put in jail by her probation officer as a punishment for not making sufficient "progress in treatment." This was a probation officer "hold," which does not require adjudication for ten working days, two weeks including weekends. Resorting to this punishment came about when the staff felt that a particular resident was intractably resistant to treatment but would respond positively to punishment, and therefore would not have to be expelled from the facility.

7. "Communication bans" can be applied to two individuals, to a group of residents, or to one resident with respect to all others. Any communication outside of formal groups is prohibited. This prohibition applies to all forms of communication including gestures, gaze, demeanor, or even bodily positioning—that is, anything that can be construed as having communicative effects.

Chapter 3

1. Revocation is an administrative proceeding held before a panel of probation/parole department supervisors. The officer in charge of the alleged violator has to make a case for revocation. If the alleged violator contests the proceeding, especially with legal representation, revocation may be denied; this makes the officer in charge look very bad. Cases for revocation in the absence of conviction of a crime are always risky business for a probation officer.

2. Probation officers have the option of placing a person in jail for up to ten working days on a "P.O. hold." After ten days the officer has to start revocation proceedings or release the person, but until that time the officer has sole responsibility.

Chapter 4

1. The amount of food stamps is estimated because this is not included in DTF's budget. The $23,000 figure is derived from that of a comparable facility that does include food stamps in its fiscal reporting.

2. The rates for outpatient counseling are from the contract with the outpatient program run by the same parent agency as DTF. These rates are comparable to other outpatient programs in the county.

3. This is based on that of the largest provider of inpatient services in the county and the only one with which the county funding agency has a purchase of service contract.

4. At one time, DTF agreed to participate in an employment program in which individuals who receive general welfare benefits are required to work at low skilled tasks in a variety of employment situations. After just a few days, it was found that the individuals sent to work at DTF caused more work than they accomplished, so DTF dropped out of the program.

5. As part of their conditions of probation, many residents were required to pay restitution. Actually, 'restitution' is a misnomer; the requirement is more like a fine because the victim of the crime never sees any of this 'restitution'; rather it goes into the public coffer.

6. That is, former prostitution customers. Women who never engaged in prostitution are not immune from such accusations. Interestingly, the image of women as prostitutes is so strong that even when one female resident returned from a pass with a noticeable amount of new clothing and cosmetics, it was assumed that her new possessions came from prostitution, when, in fact, she had shoplifted the merchandise.

7. Usually work is a moral good, although residents can be criticized for being overly zealous in their dedication to work crew assignments. Such criticisms arise when it seems that residents may be using work to avoid participating in other treatment activities, such as 'groups.'

Chapter 5

1. My impression is that such a group occurs no more than one time out of a hundred. Common opinions about such groups are negative—people (residents and staff) do not like them because they think of them as "pointless," "not going anywhere," or "a waste of time," comments that I interpret as meaning that such groups are not exciting.

Chapter 6

1. The staff members seemed to be unaware of the use of to-

bacco as a mild hallucinogen by certain people. This ignorance gives some support to Zinberg's (1984) idea of treating drug 'abuse' by making popular intoxicants subject to acculturation. One of the reasons that tobacco is not ordinarily considered a drug has to do with cultural regulatory means for its consumption; the customary form of tobacco consumption so dilutes its drug properties that it is not so conceived.

2. The reader might wonder how I could observe the difference, since I was a counselor. Especially during the last year of my tenure in the facility, I had established a reputation among residents for being a great deal more accepting than other counselors, so residents, in general, behaved less defensively in my presence. Moreover, some residents confirmed this observation when I asked them.

3. The "romantic" descriptor in this rule is so vague as to be almost impossible to interpret. The only conclusion I have been able to reach is that it is applied selectively to any suspicious behavior between men and women that cannot be otherwise categorized and thus punished.

4. I raised the issue because there had been a recent 'sex scandal' between two residents, one of whom was black and the other, white. Despite exhaustive (and exhausting) discussion of the incident in a "crisis group," little reference was made to the interracial character of their relationship. This elision was all the more striking because one of the motivations for the liaison identified by the white woman was her curiosity about having sex with a black man.

5. 'In passing' remarks or those introduced by such expressions as "oh, by the way" frequently designate repressed material in clinical psychoanalytic situations.

Chapter 7

1. Richman's study was reported in 1974, one year after the founding of the original treatment center that I studied from 1984 to 1986. Richman's study used data gathered over a twenty-five-month period from 1970 to 1972. His study is representative of those used to construct the problem of the heroin "epidemic" to formulate treatment policies at the federal level.

2. This was not the case for alcohol detoxification, which was provided by or through Community Mental Health Centers. Even at the present time, when policy for drug and alcohol treatment is directed by local government agencies, there is little support for inpatient treatment. The county funding agency that supports DTF pays for only four treatment "slots" for inpatient drug detoxification in a county with a population of about one million.

3. In the older, more Synanon-like therapeutic community communicative punishments and public confession were also used. The difference is not an either-or. The older practice used both, while the newer practice has greatly reduced shaming punishments.

REFERENCES

Agar, Michael. 1973. *Ripping and Running*. New York: Seminar Press.

Becker, Howard S. 1963. *Outsiders: Studies in the Sociology of Deviance*. New York: Macmillan.

Biernacki, Patrick. 1986. *Pathways from Heroin Addiction without Treatment*. Philadelphia: Temple University Press.

Bonnie, Richard J., and Charles H. Whitebread. 1974. *The Marihuana Conviction: The History of Marihuana Prohibition in the United States*. Charlottesville: University of Virginia Press.

Bourdieu, Pierre. 1977. *Outline of a Theory of Practice*. Translated by Richard Nice. New York: Cambridge University Press. First published 1972.

Casriel, Daniel. 1963. *So Fair a House: The Story of Synanon*. Engelwood Cliffs, N.J.: Prentice-Hall.

Casriel, Daniel, and Grover Amen. 1971. *Daytop: Three Addicts and Their Cure*. New York: Hill and Wang.

Caudill, William. 1958. *The Psychiatric Hospital as a Small Society*. Cambridge, Mass.: Harvard University Press.

Courtwright, David. 1982. *Dark Paradise: Opiate Addiction in America before 1940*. Cambridge, Mass.: Harvard University Press.

DeLeon, George. 1985. "The Therapeutic Community: Status and Evaluation." *International Journal of the Addictions* 20: 823–844.

———. 1986. "The Therapeutic Community for Substance Abuse: Perspective and Approach." In George DeLeon and James Zeigenfuss (eds.), *Therapeutic Communities for Addictions*. Springfield, Ill.: Thomas.

191

Durkheim, Emile. 1964. *The Division of Labor in Society.* Translated by George Simpson. New York: Free Press. First published 1911.

Edelman, Murray. 1974. "The Political Language of the Helping Professions." *Politics and Society* 4(3): 295–310.

Ellis, Albert. 1963. *Reason and Emotion in Psychotherapy.* New York: Lyle Stuart.

Epstein, Edward J. 1977. *Agency of Fear.* New York: Putnam.

Garfinkel, Harold. 1967. *Studies in Ethnomethodology.* Engelwood Cliffs, N.J.: Prentice-Hall.

Geertz, Clifford. 1965. "The Impact of the Concept of Culture on the Concept of Man." In John R. Platt (ed.), *New Views of Man.* Chicago: University of Chicago Press.

———. 1968. *Agricultural Involution.* Berkeley: University of California Press.

———. 1973. *The Interpretation of Cultures.* New York: Basic Books.

Goffman, Erving. 1959. *The Presentation of Self in Everyday Life.* New York: Anchor/Doubleday.

———. 1961. *Asylums.* New York: Anchor/Doubleday.

———. 1963. *Stigma.* Engelwood Cliffs, N.J.: Prentice-Hall.

Goldenweiser, Arthur. 1936. "Loose Ends of a Theory on the Individual Pattern and Involution in Primitive Society." In Robert Lowie (ed.), *Essays in Anthropology Presented to A. L. Kroeber.* Berkeley: University of California Press.

Gouldner, Alvin W. 1976. *The Dialectic of Ideology and Technology.* New York: Seabury Press.

Gramsci, Antonio. 1971. *Selections from the Prison Notebooks.* Edited and translated by Quinten Hoare and Geoffrey Smith. London: Lawrence Wishart.

Gusfield, Joseph R. 1981. *The Culture of Public Problems.* Chicago: University of Chicago Press.

Handelman, Don. 1981. "The Idea of Bureaucratic Organization." *Social Analysis* 9: 5–23.

Hawkins, J. David, and Norman Wacker. 1983. "Verbal Performances and Addict Conversion: An Interactionist Perspective on Therapeutic Communities." *Journal of Drug Issues* 13: 281–298.

———. 1986. "Side Bets and Secondary Adjustments in Therapeutic Communities." In George DeLeon and James Zeigenfuss (eds.), *Therapeutic Communities for Addictions*. Springfield, Ill.: Thomas.

Horton, Paul, and Gerald Leslie. 1970. *The Sociology of Social Problems*. 3rd edition. New York: Appleton-Century-Crofts.

Hymes, Dell. 1962. "The Ethnography of Speaking." In T. Gladwin and W. C. Sturtevant (eds.), *Anthropology and Human Behavior*. Washington, D.C.: Anthropological Society of Washington.

———. 1964. "A Perspective for Linguistic Anthropology." In Sol Tax (ed.), *Horizons of Anthropology*. Chicago: Aldine.

Inciardi, James (ed.). 1981. *The Drugs-Crime Connection*. Beverly Hills, Calif.: Sage Publications.

Johnson, Gregory. 1976. "Conversion as Cure: The Therapeutic Community and the Professional Ex-Addict." *Contemporary Drug Problems* (Summer): 187–205.

Kanter, Rosabeth Moss. 1972. *Commitment and Community*. Cambridge, Mass.: Harvard University Press.

Lasswell, Harold. 1948. "General Framework: Person, Personality, Group, Culture." In Lasswell, *The Analysis of Political Behavior*. London: Routledge and Kegan Paul. First published 1939.

Lidz, Charles W., and Andrew Walker. 1980. *Heroin, Deviance, and Morality*. Beverly Hills, Calif.: Sage Publications.

Lincoln, Bruce. 1989. *Discourse and the Construction of Society*. New York: Oxford University Press.

Mathiesen, Thomas. 1965. *The Defences of the Weak*. London: Tavistock.

Maultsby, Maxie C. 1975. *Help Yourself to Happiness*. New York: Institute for Rational Living.

McCoy, Alfred. 1972. *The Politics of Heroin in Southeast Asia*. New York: Harper and Row.

Michaels, Robert J. 1987. "The Market for Heroin before and after Legalization." In Ronald Hamowy (ed.), *Dealing with Drugs*. Lexington Mass.: Lexington Books.

Miller, Eleanor. 1986. *Street Woman*. Philadelphia: Temple University Press.

Moore, Mark H. 1977. *Buy and Bust*. Lexington, Mass.: Lexington Books.

Musto, David. 1973. *The American Disease: Origins of Narcotic Control*. New Haven, Conn.: Yale University Press.

Myerhoff, Barbara. 1982. "Life History among the Elderly: Performance, Visibility, and Re-Membering." In Jay Ruby (ed.), *A Crack in the Mirror*. Philadelphia: University of Pennsylvania Press.

———. 1986. "'Life Not Death in Venice': Its Second Life." In Victor Turner and Edward Bruner (eds.), *The Anthropology of Experience*. Urbana: University of Illinois Press.

Page, Richard C., and Sam Mitchell. 1988. "The Effects of Two Theraputic Communities on Illicit Drug Users between Six Months and One Year after Treatment." *International Journal of the Addictions* 23: 591–601.

Preble, Edward, and John Casey. 1969. "Taking Care of Business: The Heroin User's Life on the Streets." *International Journal of the Addictions* 4: 1–24.

Reasons, Charles. 1974. "The Politics of Drugs: An Inquiry in the Sociology of Social Problems." *Sociological Quarterly* 15: 381–404.

Richman, Alex. 1977. "Ecological Studies of Narcotic Addiction." In *The Epidemiology of Drug Abuse*. NIDA Research Monograph 10. Rockville, Md.: U.S. Department of Health and Human Services. First published 1974.

Rosenbaum, Marsha. 1981. "Women Addicts' Experience of the Heroin World." *Urban Life* 10(1): 65–91.

Scott, James C. 1985. *Weapons of the Weak*. New Haven, Conn.: Yale University Press.

Simpson, D. Dwayne. 1984. "National Treatment System Evaluation Based on the Drug Abuse Reporting Program (DARP) Followup Research." In Frank Tims and Jacqueline Luford (eds.), *Drug Abuse Treatment Evaluation Strategies, Programs, and Prospects*. NIDA Research Monograph 51. Rockville, Md.: U.S. Department of Health and Human Services.

Spicer, Edward. 1971. "Persistent Cultural Systems." *Science* 174: 795–800.

Stack, Carol B. 1974. *All Our Kin: Strategies for Survival in a Black Community*. New York: Harper Colophon Books.

Stolcke, Verena. 1984. "The Exploitation of Family Morality: Labor Systems and Family Structure in Sao Paulo Coffee Plantations, 1850–1979." In Raymond T. Smith (ed.), *Kinship Ideology and Practice in Latin America*. Chapel Hill: University of North Carolina Press.

Sugarman, Barry. 1974. *Daytop Village: A Therapeutic Community*. New York: Holt, Rinehart and Winston.

Sutter, Alan. 1966. "The World of the Righteous Dope Fiend." *Issues in Criminology* 2(2): 177–221.

Thompson, E. P. 1978. "Folklore, Anthropology, and Social History." *Indian Historical Review* 3: 247–266.

Trebach, Arnold. 1987. *The Great Drug War*. New York: Macmillan.

Turner, Victor. 1974. *Dramas, Fields, and Metaphors*. Ithaca: Cornell University Press.

———. 1957. *Schism and Continuity in an African Society*. Manchester: University of Manchester Press.

Valentine, Bettylou. 1978. *Hustling and Other Hard Work*. New York: Free Press.

Weppner, Robert. 1983. *The Untherapeutic Community*. Lincoln: University of Nebraska Press.

Willis, Paul. 1981. *Learning to Labor*. New York: Columbia University Press. First published 1977.

Wurmser, Leon. 1978. *The Hidden Dimension*. New York: Jason Aronson.

Yablonsky, Lewis. 1965. *The Tunnel Back*. New York: Macmillan.

———. 1989. *The Therapeutic Community*. New York: Gardner Press.

Zinberg, Norman. 1984. *Drug, Set, and Setting*. New Haven, Conn.: Yale University Press.

INDEX